THE CRUSADES

THE CRUSADES

HISTORY & MYTHS REVEALED

MICHAEL PAINE

FALL RIVER PRESS

This 2009 edition published by Fall River Press
by arrangement with Alexian Limited

Designed & produced by Alexian Limited

Art director: Terry Jeavons

Designer: Andrew Milne

Editor: Fiona Biggs

Picture research: Vanessa Fletcher

Fall River Press
122 Fifth Avenue
New York, NY 10011

ISBN -13: 978 -1 - 4351 - 0820 - 2

Printed and bound in Singapore

10   9   8   7   6   5   4   3   2   1

PICTURE CREDITS

Contents

Foreword

From the perspective of the twenty-first century, it is difficult to imagine a time in the Middle East when people across the whole region lived together in harmony, irrespective of race or religion. This had in fact been the case for many years, that is until the Church in Europe launched a series of bloody crusades, which were to have a cataclysmic effect on the people of the region, the effects of which are still being felt to this day.

The historical crusades also mark an interesting and important period in the development of the European nation-state, and are an early stage in the involvement of Europe in the affairs of the rest of the world—almost invariably for political and economic advantage. In later centuries many of the states of Europe became heads of rich and powerful empires, and this wealth and power was due in large part to their exploitation of much of the rest of the world. So we can perhaps view the Crusades as the first tentative steps toward these European empires.

Critically, however, Crusaders saw themselves as doing God's work, just as those who followed much later saw themselves bringing *civilization* to Africa, India, and the Far East. Inevitably, economic benefits accompanied

▶ Duke Leopold the Glorious of Austria (1176–1230) enters Vienna on his return from the Fifth Crusade.

▶ Vanquished Muslim armies in flight from the Christian invader became a popular theme in the West in the era of the Crusades.

both undertakings. And despite the large cost in men and goods, it has been argued that the wealth coming into the Italian city-states during the Crusades, through both increased trade and conquest, was a major factor in bringing forward the period of Italian Renaissance.

Despite the enormous passage of time, which might be expected to dull the memory of the human cost of the Crusades to the Middle East, or reduce the anger at their memory, the image of the Crusades as the start of a long process of exploitation, of rule by the West of the rest of the world cannot be ignored, and brings them ever closer to the modern era.

Some conquests, some wars, are more easily forgiven than others. The invasions of much of Europe by the Romans, of England by the Vikings and then by the Normans all ended with assimilation. Indeed, the great success of the Roman Empire can be attributed to the manner in which the Romans consciously sought to merge their own culture with the cultures of those they had conquered. The Crusades were to be different. They were firmly based, as were the later imperialist conquests, upon ideas of segregation and the imposition of one belief system. The Crusaders, while of different races and languages, were unified by one thing—their Christian faith; and there was no possibility of a compromise here. One was either a Christian or one was not. This was to be a defining moment in the historical development of the relationship between Europe and the rest of the world. On one side are the Europeans, who are Christians, and against them are *others*, who are seen as inferior because of the very thing that most identified them—their religious belief.

A third development has helped the word retain its potency. The establishment of the state of Israel in 1948, while bearing no relationship to the acts and intents of the Crusaders, is still, in the eyes of some, a symbol of a loss that resonates with the crusading period. Israel was formed subsequent to the brief British rule of Palestine, which came under its control after the First World War, following centuries of rule by the Ottoman Empire, and its main foreign source of financial support in the present day is the United States of America. To some Muslims these facts again echo and recall the involvement of the West in the Crusades of the Middle Ages. So, to this day, the word crusade remains extraordinarily potent.

Every war has its reasons, its justifications, and its legacies. One can never entirely disentangle the past from the present with ease, so that any book that brings a historical period to life does so in part by linking it to the present. Long dead figures come alive when we see their similarities to us; when their motivations are ones that we can understand. Our understanding of the terror felt by the inhabitants of the Crusader states toward the Assassins—the fear that at any moment, in a public place, careless of their own survival, an Assassin might strike—is

grimly brought to life in our world by today's terrorist attacks. No doubt in a few hundred years historians will look back and judge whether we too are living today in crusading times.

▶ The Old Man of the Mountains, the leader of the Assassins, allows his men to enjoy the delights of Paradise, the reward for their successful attacks on the Infidel.

1 The Islamic World and the East

THE FABLED BYZANTINE EMPIRE HAD A CULTURE AND SOPHISTICATION THAT WAS UNHEARD OF IN WESTERN EUROPE IN THE DARK AGES. FOR YEARS, THOSE OF DIFFERENT FAITHS LIVED IN HARMONY ALONGSIDE EACH OTHER WITHIN THE TERRITORIES OF THE EMPIRE. HOWEVER, WHEN ISLAM BEGAN TO DIVERGE, IT BECAME A THREAT TO BYZANTINE CHRISTIANS.

Introduction

Centuries of dust covered the fabulous gardens of Haroun al-Rashid, Caliph of Baghdad, Commander of the Faithful. The splendor of the barges that conveyed him down the Tigris at night with his faithful wazir, Jafar; the anonymous walks with his sword-bearer, Masrur, among his subjects in the morning market place—these tales were told by storytellers on the streets of medieval Damascus and Cairo, and in the souks of Baghdad itself. Haroun, like his Frankish contemporary Charlemagne, was a figure who slipped out from between the covers of history and passed into myth. In these stories, eventually to make their way into the *Alf Layla wa-Layla*—frequently translated into English as the Arabian Nights, although a more literal translation would be The Thousand Nights and One Night—the political security of al-Rashid's reign appears against the opulent backdrop of palaces and merchant caravans and endless, lush detail. Whatever the realities of life at the end of the eighth century A.D. Under Abbasid rule, it was, in retrospect, a golden age. To an audience in the schismatic and politically-divided Middle East of the eleventh century it would not have been difficult to accept the wealth of these tales as the fruit of a Muslim world unified under one leader sanctioned by God: the Dar al-Islam.

For the divided state of Islam is at the heart of the early successes of the Crusades. The first three centuries after the irruption of Islam among the Arabs and Bedouin of the Arabian peninsula had seen it spread rapidly across a large part of the ancient world. Most of Arabia had converted by the death of Mohammed in A.D. 632. Those old empires, Byzantine and Sassanian, which had spent so long quarreling over their shared Near-Eastern hinterlands, were in turn driven back by these converts. Jerusalem surrendered in 638. By 640 the Romans had lost Syria. Egypt had fallen by 646. By 651 the last Sassanian Emperor—Yazdegerd III—and the four-hundred-year-old empire he had ruled had passed into history. Territories fell in turn as North Africa—the Maghrib—was overrun up to the very gateway to Western Europe. By the middle of the eighth century, even Iberia (modern Spain and Portugal) was occupied by an army composed of Arabs and the Muslim converts of the Maghrib, the Berbers. Occasional raiding parties came over the Pyrenees. The significance of the defeat of one such party in 732 by Charles Martel—known as Charles the Hammer—grew with the telling, until it became known as the epic battle that saved Europe from a final and complete conquest by the Infidel. But apart from these raids, this was the Islamic world, the Dar al-Islam, unrolled across the map as far as it would go.

▼ The legendary caliph of Baghdad, Haroun al-Rashid, receives envoys from Charlemagne in 786.

The empire is challenged

The conquest of the Maghrib had involved the annexation of Byzantine cities such as Carthage. Beginning with the conquest of Syria in the first half of the seventh century, Muslim forces worried away at the eastern half of the Byzantine Empire for the next 80 years, laying siege to the capital, Byzantium, in 674 and again in 717. The earlier siege was finally repulsed after four years, partly due to the Byzantines' unique weapon, Greek fire—a liquid whose recipe has been lost but that can perhaps best be described as medieval napalm. The Byzantine Empire, which had thrived and spread across the coastal areas of the Mediterranean as a consequence of its uncontested command of that sea, now found itself increasingly challenged by both Islamic navies and Islamic pirates. It was, in part, the contest between these two great cultures, Islam and Byzantium, that would eventually lead to the First Crusade.

▼ Greek fire was effectively used by the Byzantines as a weapon both on land and at sea.

Who were the Byzantines? The name itself is slightly decep-tive. Their origin was Roman, and their story is in part the answer to the question of what happened to the Roman Empire. The origin of Byzantium itself was a Greek colony founded in the eighth century B.C. For hundreds of years it remained a provincial center, rising to prominence when the first Christian Roman emperor, Constantine I, on ascending to power in A.D. 324, chose to make it, rather than Rome, his capital. This new capital city soon took on its founder's name, and thus was Constantinople born. As an imperial capital, the fortified city grew rapidly both in size and strength. Time passed, and the empire split in two: tucked away at the edge of Europe, the Roman Empire of the East was well placed to avoid the barbarian hordes that finally overwhelmed Rome.

As the empire of the West receded into memory, the East gradu-ally found its own path of development. By the medieval period its blend of Eastern cultural sophistication, the particular route taken by its Christianity in terms of both ritual and belief, and its Roman inheritance had justified a new description by historians as Byzantine. This empire would become a shining beacon at the edge of Dark Age Europe, a very real link with the Roman world that would last until Constantinople was conquered by the Ottoman Turks in 1453. The Byzantines may have seen themselves as the continuation of Rome, and perhaps as the safeguard and continuation of all that was truly civilized in Rome. They were maintaining Europe's great old civili-zation. However, this cultural gap would become more pronounced with the passing centuries, and their physical position at the edge of the continent merely rendered them increasingly foreign, until they were viewed as non-European by the European kingdoms that came into being as a result of the barbarian invasions. Ironically, it was only toward the end of their empire, with the rebirth of interest in the

▲ The first Christian Roman emperor, Constantine, who gave his name to the city of Constantinople.

classical world in Italy that is known as the Renaissance, that the lonely light kept burning by Byzantium throughout the long centuries of the Dark Ages finally spread back to the old territories of Rome.

The empire radiated out from the hub of Constantinople. At its core were always Asia Minor and Thracian Greece, below the Danube. Added to these lands were much of the North African coast, Egypt, Dalmatia (modern Yugoslavia), southern Italy, and Sicily. At its eastern marches were the Sassanids; to the west, the tribes of the Balkans. A constant feature was the pressure from nomadic peoples moving from Asia into Europe, and driving forward those they found before them. In the east the replacement of the Sassanids by the Arabs simply increased the difficulties of the Byzantines.

The siege of 717, however, represented the high-water mark of Islamic ambition where Constantinople was concerned. The Arabs were again repulsed and, while they continued to make incursions into

◄ A victorious Mahomet II enters Constantinople at the head of his troops.

◄ A Western artist's impression of the city of Constantinople, center of the powerful Byzantine Empire.

▶ The interior of the Great Mosque at Cordoba, built in 786–87 by Adb al-Rahman I, and enlarged three times by his successors.

▼ A battle between Crusaders and Muslims, taken from the *Roman de Godefroi de Bouillon*, an account of the exploits of one of the foremost leaders of the First Crusade.

Byzantine territory, they became increasingly fragmented within their ranks. The Umayyad dynasty had held total control of the Islamic world from 661 to 750. The subsequent rise of the Abbasids still left them the emirate of Cordoba, comprising most of modern Spain and Portugal. With the ascent of the Abbasids the capital moved from Damascus to Baghdad. By the tenth century the Abbasids, too, were in decline, with many autonomous Muslim states appearing across the Maghrib and the Near East. The Byzantines made the most of this political disarray. The Abbasids held power to the east; a rival dynasty, the Fatamids, had the Maghrib. From 945 the Byzantines marched out under a variety of rulers and took back many of the Levantine cities that were under the control of the minor Muslim rulers, successively confronting the Fatamids and Abbasids.

▲ The Mosque of Omar in Jerusalem. The site of the Temple of Jerusalem can be seen in the middle ground.

◀ The modern-day city of Istanbul in Turkey, formerly Constantinople.

By the eleventh century, there was a general truce in place between the three major forces. As would often prove the case later on, the enmity was actually greater between the two Islamic sides than between either of them and the Byzantines. Jerusalem had been under Islamic control ever since it had surrendered to the Caliph Omar in 638. The Christians there, as was commonly the case elsewhere, enjoyed reasonable treatment under the Muslims. The latter were prepared to tolerate Christian and Jewish religious practice, because they regarded the followers of these two religions as *ahl al-kitab*, people of the Book. Indeed, all three religions were connected. Just as Christianity had its roots in Judaism, so Muslims accorded Jesus the position of prophet—adherents of all three faiths, in essence, worshiped the same god. This relationship meant that Christians often and easily converted to Islam—it was not difficult to argue that the latter religion was a more advanced stage of the former.

The tolerance shown to these faiths by the Muslims was not with-out cost—literally so. A tax, *jizyah*, was payable by all who were allowed to follow these divergent beliefs. It was this tax, and the obvious advantages of following a religion that was indivisible from the political power, that provided an additional strong incentive to convert when spiritual arguments proved insufficient. The enormous expansion in the numbers of believers that resulted from these prag-matic conversions brought a cultural and social variety that both strengthened and weakened the Islamic world. In the short term an immediate problem was the loss of tax revenue. In the long term the greater diversity in backgrounds between Muslims proved more problematic. Factionalism had been a problem when the religion had been an entirely Arabic affair. The scope for division was very much greater when so many different cultures now described themselves as Islamic. Islam's great strength in its early period of conquest had been its unity—Muslims had shared beliefs and a shared culture. Now dif-ferent communities within Islam had their own interests to promote and protect.

▼ Christian pilgrims arrive at the Church of the Holy Sepulcher in Jerusalem. Christian practice was tolerated by the Muslims before the Crusades to the Holy Land began.

These inner tensions were not unique to Islam: the Byzantine Empire was frequently riven by its own brands of dissent. The most notorious was the enor-mous controversy that raged over whether or not religious iconography was acceptable. For most of the eighth cen-tury there was strife between those who used icons and those who were fervently opposed to them. Alongside these social conflicts were the more per-

sonal disputes: the family quarrels and treacheries that had so often bedeviled the Caesars were not unfamiliar to their Byzantine descendants. But not everything was about differences. The blend of Greek, Roman, Sassanid, and Persian civilizations existing in the East made for a sophisticated culture that was common to both Byzantine and Muslim. While the Byzantines preserved Roman and Greek civilization the scholars of Islam prevented the loss of much ancient Greek thought and, in addition, had their own contributions to make—in the field of mathematics, for instance. Much divided the two civilizations but much united them, too. In comparison the societies of Western Europe at this time were indeed those of barbarians, living in colder climates at the edge of the world.

So the condition of Christians in the Holy Land in the eleventh century was by no means intolerable. True, Jerusalem was still held by the Fatamids. In practice, however, the tolerance shown toward many of the differing Christian cults in the East was greater than they would have received from their own brethren in religion. Both the Byzantine Orthodox Church and the Roman Catholic Church attempted at times to wipe out divergent practices and beliefs; Muslim protected these Eastern Christians from such attempts. Yet, against the occasional desire of the Orthodox Church to control their practices, a strong and Christian empire at the border of the Islamic world must also have reassured Christians living under Muslim rule to some extent. While the Muslims tolerated them life was not that bad, and, if things took a turn for the worse, they didn't have far to go to seek sanctuary. This balance and understanding between the two civilizations, though far from secure, contributed to a peace that benefited more than just the people of both empires. The situation was sufficiently secure for pilgrims from distant Europe to journey to Jerusalem and the other holy sites in relative safety. Yet something was about to upset the balance.

The Seljuk Turks, coming out of Turkestan in central Asia, were recent converts to Islam. Turks had featured as Abbasid mercenaries for a while, with a fearsome reputation. Under their leader, Tughril Beg, they had supplanted Abbasid rule. After Tughril Beg's death in 1063 his successor, Alp Arslan, embarked on a series of campaigns

◀ The Dark Ages in Europe was a period when Islamic scholarship flowered. The ninth-century Muslim alchemist Jabir Ibn Haiyan is regarded by many as the father of modern chemistry.

▼ The Seljuk sultan, Alp Arslan, surrounded by his courtiers.

against the Byzantines. After a number of other victories, the Turks conquered Armenia, an independent Christian state that had recently gone over to the Byzantines. The stage was set for a decisive confrontation between Christian and Turk.

It came in 1071. The Battle of Manzikert was one of the darkest days for the Byzantine Empire. A large Byzantine army, which included many mercenaries—Normans, Vikings, Slavs, and even Turks (an unwise addition to the forces since they defected at a crucial moment toward the end of the conflict)—was comprehensively crushed. The emperor, Romanus Diogenes, was captured. While the Turkish command did not seek immediately to press the advantage, the opportunity was later taken up by others—nomadic Turks seeking land on which to settle. Led by Suleiman ibn Kutulmish, they began to make inroads into Byzantine territory in Asia Minor from 1073. Jerusalem had been taken from the Fatamids in 1071. Turkish adventurers sprang up everywhere, taking land from either side. Chaos ensued. The steady stream of pilgrims from Europe now dried up— those travelers who dared to make their way over the traditional land routes frequently fell prey to groups of marauding bandits.

After Manzikert, there was feuding among the ruling classes of Constantinople until the emergence of Alexius Comnenus, who saw clearly that his most pressing task was to bring back the empire from the brink of destruction. With the Turks to the east, the Bulgars to the west, and the recent loss of southern Italy to the Normans, the empire was in an perilous position. As he played off minor Turkish chiefs against each other in a struggle to ensure the empire's survival, Alexius was all too aware of the weaknesses of his position, and of the vulnerability of his empire. Although skilled diplomacy could keep his enemies at each other's throats for the time being, the solution, as he saw it, was strength in the form of arms and armies to ensure Byzantium's long-term survival. But where was an army to be found?

◀ The Battle of Manzikert in 1071, a decisive victory for the Turks.

▼ Emperor Alexius I Comnenus, who reigned from 1081 to 1118, was committed to ensuring the survival of the Empire.

2 The First Crusade

IN 1095, THE FIRST CALL TO ARMS IN A CRUSADE AGAINST THE INFIDEL WAS ENTHUSIASTICALLY RECEIVED BY THE POPULATIONS AND NOBILITY OF EUROPE.

Introduction

When the request for aid in the struggle against the Infidel reached Rome, it was not dismissed out of hand. The Muslims' conquest of Iberia, and their forays across the Pyrenees, had proved to be a thorn in the side of the West. Numerous campaigns had been launched against them; some had even involved the Byzantines working alongside Western Europeans. Rome itself, having previously been sacked by Islamic forces, was aware of the threat that they could present. With their command of the Mediterranean, Muslims were able to establish bases in Provence and southern Italy from which they could strike at will. Pilgrims returning from the Holy Land told of the dreadful conditions there. Islamic aggression seemed to be a threat both at home and abroad.

In the Western theater of conflict, the pope had already encouraged the cooperation of French and Italian nobles in coming to the aid of beleaguered Christian Spain. From 1063

▼ The Moors hand over the keys to the city of Granada on January 2nd, 1492, after years of war against Christian Spain.

expeditions were launched, often to little effect. The *Reconquista*—as the attempt to reclaim Spain from the Moors was called—would take the better part of eight hundred years to achieve its aim, from its beginnings at the Battle of Covadonga in 718 to the fall of Granada, the last Iberian Arab state, in 1492.

In 1095, however, a reclaimed Spain was centuries away. At the great Church council of Piacenza, Pope Urban II received ambassadors from Emperor Alexius. What messages they delivered are unknown. Alexius was making some progress in his fight against the Muslims and it is probable that he used a combination of his successes and the cost to the West should he

▲ The Alhambra Palace in Granada, court of the ruling Moors, built during the fourteenth century as part of a fortress complex.

fail as leverage to extract help from the pope. The model existed in Spain, haphazard though it was, for uniting Christian forces against unbelievers. Many personal reasons for providing help must have occurred to Urban. What greater achievement could mark his papacy than a colossal campaign to free the sacred sites of the Holy Land from the Infidel? What effect might Western involvement have on the possibilities of rapprochement with that "dissident" Eastern half of the Church? Regardless of the details, the ideas behind the Crusade—the taking up of arms against Christ's opponents, the great unifying cause in a Christendom split by petty disagreements and squabbles—took root in his mind between Piacenza and the first official announcement of the Crusade, at the Council of Clermont, France. This was to have been a council concerned with other matters. Alongside the launch of the Crusades, the Truce of God—a policy seeking to promote peace between Christian leaders in Europe—was strongly advocated. But Clermont would always be remembered as the beginning of the Crusades.

The call to arms

On Tuesday, November 27th, 1095, before a huge, rapt crowd outside the city of Clermont, Pope Urban II announced the call to arms. His speech, legend has it, was interrupted by shouts of "Deus lo volt!" (God wills it!). Apparently spontaneously, those present, both rich and poor, in an enormous outpouring of emotion, offered to take up the pope's call. Despite the popular reception of his plan, there was a problem—Urban had not signed up any leading members of the nobility to his cause. He had an experienced and capable cleric, the bishop of Le Puy, who would take charge of the crusade on behalf of the Church, but who were the men who would organize and lead the armies?

This issue was quickly resolved. Alongside the noble intent to fight for Christ, the spiritual pull of the call to arms, and the promise of reward in the hereafter, a more prosaic and more secular reason encouraged young nobles to go: primogeniture. On the death of a male member of the nobility his property and wealth would, in most of Europe, pass to his eldest son. This meant that after exhausting that pool of fighting men who were motivated by faith, or by the desire for battle and for glory, there were many ambitious young men who saw the opportunity of making their fortune under cover of doing good. Living in an age without newspapers or television, their prime source of information about the Holy Land was the Bible. Thoughts of the Land of Milk and Honey must have been to the forefront of the minds of many of them. What contact they had had with Islam was enough to indicate that this was a rich and sophisticated civilization, and the chance to take the fight to Islamic shores, after years of suffering Muslim raids, must have appealed. Life was hard enough at home for many of them. Could the East be any worse?

▲ ▶ Pope Urban II, instigator of the First Crusade, announces his call to arms to a huge crowd outside the city of Clermont in 1095. The enthusiastic popular response was soon followed by the commitment of many young noblemen to the cause.

Nobles soon came forward to sign up for the cause. Chief among them were Raymond, Count of Toulouse, and Stephen, Count of Blois; Robert, Duke of Normandy, and Robert, Count of Flanders; Bohemond of Taranto and his nephew Tancred; and the brothers Baldwin, Eustace, and Godfrey from Lorraine. Meanwhile, more volunteers poured forth from among the poorer members of society. While Urban had instructed his bishops to preach the message, certain members of the Church went farther than he would have anticipated. Indigent, wandering zealots like Peter the Hermit moved through towns and villages, whipping up a frenzy with their preaching. The common people were spellbound. The various spontaneous movements inspired by these preachers became known as the People's Crusade. The official Crusade was still in preparation when two huge rabbles, the first led by Walter the Penniless, the second by Peter the

▶ Godfrey of Bouillon, Raymond of Toulouse, Bohemond of Taranto, and his nephew Tancred, four of the most important leaders of the First Crusade.

◄ Walter the Penniless, a mendicant preacher, whips up a frenzy of fervor for the Crusade.

▶ Peter the Hermit traveled through towns and villages, encouraging support for the Crusade among the common people.

Hermit, set off for Constantinople. The lack of professional leadership soon became apparent. Supplies for the journey had been the last things on the volunteers' minds and, as they marched through Hungary and Bulgaria, they were forced to relieve the inhabitants of what they needed. Having suffered the depredations of Walter's followers, towns and villages barely had time to recover before Peter's even larger crowd appeared in their wake. From the point of view of these masses of impoverished people, driven by a fanatical desire to fight for God, the farms and the herds of sheep or cattle that appeared in their path must have seemed providential. The feelings of the farmers or shepherds might have been somewhat less Christian. It was reported that an argument that began over a pair of shoes in Hungary led to a conflict resulting in thousands of deaths.

What Alexius made of this rude army when the two forces reached Constantinople has not been recorded. It could hardly have been what he had been expecting, much less what he had been hoping for. After spending some time in the capital—where they helped themselves to whatever came to hand, even the lead from church roofs—they crossed the Bosphorus. Though he probably had a sense of hopelessness, Alexius must also have been pleased to see them go. The absence of informed leadership, general order, any kind of clear intent, or, presumably, much ability to communicate with those they met led to unsurprising results. In Asia Minor they wreaked havoc on anything and anyone unfortunate enough to lie in their path: Muslims, Christians, young and old, men and women. Most were butchered, their belongings taken and sold when the opportunity or need arose—Greek sailors in coastal ports are supposed to have done well out of this trade. The local Turkish ruler soon reacted to this unholy force. A sizeable group who had taken over the castle of Xerigordon were besieged, reduced through thirst to drinking the blood of their mounts and their own urine, and then forced to renounce their faith or embrace death. Those who converted to Islam spent the rest of their lives as slaves.

▼ A group of Crusaders come upon the bodies of some of Peter the Hermit's pilgrims.

The rest of the disorderly army was caught out outside the town of Civetot. A minority managed to escape with their lives; a few were captured as slaves. Peter the Hermit had returned to Constantinople a little while before. Having been instrumental in leading tens of thousands to their deaths, and probably a little puzzled by his lack of success, he now sat back and waited for reinforcements to arrive.

As their preparations reached completion, the separate armies of the First Crusade made their way toward the East, each under separate command.

Godfrey of Bouillon crosses the Bosphorus in 1097 together with his brother, "Baldwin".

Godfrey of Bouillon crosses the Bosphorus in 1097, together with his brother, Baldwin.

Arriving at Constantinople, they felt the same cultural queasiness that barbarians traditionally experience at the courts of more advanced civilizations. The average soldier must have found it difficult to square his impoverished journey with the conspicuous wealth of these people he had been called upon to "help out" in their struggle against the Infidel. In addition, gratitude must have been in short supply among the Byzantines, after their experiences with their earlier visitors. The Western leaders, however, were impressed and, for the main part, won over by Alexius and his generous gifts—gifts that sweetened the bitter pill of swearing an oath of allegiance to a foreign power. With a complement of Byzantines, the various forces and their leaders moved across the Bosphorus.

Their first act was to attempt to take the town of Nicaea. This was the first battle against the enemy. Troops sent by the local sultan to relieve the siege fought a pitched battle with the Crusaders, who put up a resistance that the Turks would not have expected after their previous encounter with Peter the Hermit's men. In the end, the Turks fled.

The Christians were jubilant, despite heavy losses. The inhabitants of Nicaea, had they been in any doubt as to who were the victors, had their hopes swiftly dashed when a barrage of severed Turkish heads was hurled over the walls by the rejoicing Crusaders. When it became clear that the emperor was bringing up support, the town bowed to the inevitable. In June, 1097, Nicaea was surrendered to the Crusaders, who, in turn, presented it to Alexius. The Christian troops were no doubt displeased at the lost opportunity for pillaging. Their leaders received gold; they had to be content with an extra meal.

While passing Dorylaeum, the first major test of the Crusaders' mettle occurred when they were ambushed by a sizeable force of Turks. The fact that these Crusaders were of a very different sort from the disorganized peasant troops led by Peter the Hermit had not yet sunk in, and

Jubilant Crusaders throw the heads of their enemies over the ramparts of the city of Nicaea.

Survivors bury the dead after the hard-won Crusader victory in the Battle of Dorylaeum.

Baldwin of Boulogne entering Edessa in February 1098. He was welcomed by the populace and soon assumed sole leadership of the city.

the Turkish forces still expected an easy victory. As it was, the Crusaders bravely held their ground, before breaking the Turkish attack.

The army continued toward the southeast. Harried sporadically as it passed through the Taurus Mountains—losing many men—it finally arrived at the outskirts of the great city of Antioch. Part of the army, under Baldwin of Boulogne, had parted from the main army before this. How Baldwin justified his actions is unknown. Whatever his excuse, he gradually moved southeast toward the Armenian city of Edessa as the rest of the Crusaders moved southwest with the aim of taking Antioch. The Armenians of Edessa had been displaced by Turkish forces from their homeland to the northeast. Now they existed as a Byzantine client state, a buffer between the Byzantine coastal territory and the Arab interior. Though the support the Armenians received from Constantinople was essential to their continued survival they resented being used. The differences between Armenian and Orthodox practices and beliefs became another source of tension. But the Christians from the West had yet to sully their reputation in Armenian eyes. Baldwin's appearance was thus greeted very favorably and, from being the leader of a potential mercenary force against the Emir of Mosul—who was rumored to be gathering an army to relieve Antioch that would destroy Edessa in passing—he soon rose to become first co-regent and then sole leader of Edessa. Striking out on his own had clearly been advantageous to the ambitious Baldwin.

In October preparations for the siege had been made at Antioch. The city's massive walls made it clear that it would not fall easily. The success that the Crusaders had experienced so far had not prepared them for the slow siege that ensued. Days turned into weeks, and then into months.

The troops grew steadily more despondent, and news of Baldwin's easy success would not necessarily—in the light of his decision to set off independently—have cheered them.

More and more seemed to go against them. Supplies for the army were initially gathered from the lands around the city. As time went on, they were forced to forage farther and farther afield. Where was the support Alexius had promised? The hoped-for supplies did not arrive, and the support anticipated from the ships of mercantile Italian cities, such as Genoa, now that a section of the Holy Land coast was free of Muslim control, also failed to appear. Antioch itself had a substantial Christian population—the besiegers must have expected some contribution from these locals toward their "liberation." The divisive nature of sectarian Christianity worked against the Crusaders here. In Edessa, the Armenians welcomed Baldwin precisely because he wasn't Orthodox. Here, the Syrian Christians had no desire to place themselves under either Orthodox or Catholic hegemony. Their estimation that their Turkish masters were probably the ones under whom they would enjoy the greater religious freedom was probably an astute one. To the Crusaders this must have seemed to lie somewhere between treachery and apostasy. Initially, with expectations of support in the air, the Crusaders were unwilling to press the conflict until at least some troops had materialized. News of this soon got back to Yaghi-Siyan, governor of Antioch. Encouraged, he authorized night raids on Crusader encampments, more for the purpose of reducing morale than for any real military gain. The city itself was safeguarded by the skill and technology of previous Byzantine regimes, whose experience of withstanding aggressors had made them past masters of the art.

◀ The Crusaders retreat from the walls of Antioch after a failed attempt to breach its defenses.

With the onset of winter food became scarce. The weather grew colder and it rained relentlessly. There was even an earthquake. To keep the Orthodox Christians in order, the Turks imprisoned their most senior churchman in a cage swinging from the outer walls of the city.

There was the occasional bit of good news—the establishment of a chain of supply of food from Cyprus, and the fact that each new Islamic force that appeared on the scene to relieve the siege was driven back in disarray, gave some cause for hope. Spring of 1098 saw an improvement in the weather. Some support from Constantinople would turn up in the occasional trading ship from Europe that had stopped off on the way to the Holy Land, still carrying pilgrims. Requests for more help continued to be sent back to the emperor via these travelers. It was not long, however, before disillusioned Crusaders themselves were accompanying these requests, on their way back to Europe. By the time Alexius himself finally set out with a group to aid them, he encountered a cheerless Stephen of Blois on the road, leading a force of despondent Frenchmen whose tale that all was lost managed to convince the emperor to turn back.

Ironically, it was at this point that a breakthrough was made. Bohemond had been cultivating traitors within and one of them finally paid off. On June 3rd, 1098, the great outer walls of Antioch were breached and the Crusaders broke through, slaughtering every Muslim they found. The homes of Muslim and Christian alike were looted, the Crusaders taking the opportunity to avenge themselves on their coreligionists for their lack of Christian solidarity.

Unfortunately, the inner citadel of the city still held out. For its defenders, the killing of their fellow townsfolk was a fairly convincing argument in favor of continued resistance. This was not the only problem faced by the Crusaders. By this time, a sizeable force

▼ The discovery of the lance reputed to have pierced the side of Christ during the Crucifixion encouraged the Crusaders to continue with their long siege.

of Turks had arrived under Kerbogha of Mosul with the aim of relieving the siege. News of their approach had steeled the resolve of the citadel's inhabitants. The Westerners suddenly found themselves caught like rats in a looted city, with the corpses of their victims rotting in the ever-increasing summer heat. Their situation seemed hopeless, with enemies before them and at their backs.

Then their fortunes began to change once more—this time for the better. The mood of the Crusaders started to lift after a sequence

▼ Robert of Normandy in battle during the siege of Antioch. The desertion by part of the Turkish army caused panic among the ranks and helped the Crusaders to achieve victory.

▲ Bohemond's army is attacked by the Turkish army as it crosses the River Wardar. The defeat of these Turks contributed to the fall of Antioch.

of holy signs. Acting on the visions of a peasant, they had found the lance that was supposed to have pierced Christ's side under St. Peter's Cathedral. Other visions contributed to the belief that a breakthrough was just around the corner. On the Turkish side, the struggle to hold together the various forces began to show. On June 28th the armies of the Crusaders rode out, temporarily abandoning the siege, and defeated their divided opponents. The desertion by part of the Turkish army caused panic to spread among the other Turks. Rumors of visions of knights on white horses led by saints spread inspiration through the ranks of the Crusaders as they fought and few of the Turks survived—many of those who escaped the battlefield were caught and killed by vengeful locals.

Watching this rout from the hill inside the city, the inhabitants of Antioch realized that the situation was hopeless. Arrangements were made to surrender to Bohemond of Taranto. With Raymond too ill to protest, Bohemond grasped the opportunity presented—in spite of the oaths the nobles had made to hand over the recaptured city to the emperor. When they heard later of Alexius' decision to turn back while the siege was taking place, it confirmed their decision not to return Antioch to the Byzantines, and reaffirmed all the doubts they had had about them. But their anger was not reserved for the empire alone.

Stephen of Blois' reputation, which had already been stained by his decision to leave, was reduced to shreds after the Crusaders heard that it was partly because of his intervention that Alexius had decided to pull back his reinforcements. However, even the knowledge of Stephen's role was not sufficient to redeem Alexius in the eyes of the other Crusaders.

▼ This fifteenth-century French illuminated manuscript depicts the siege of Antioch.

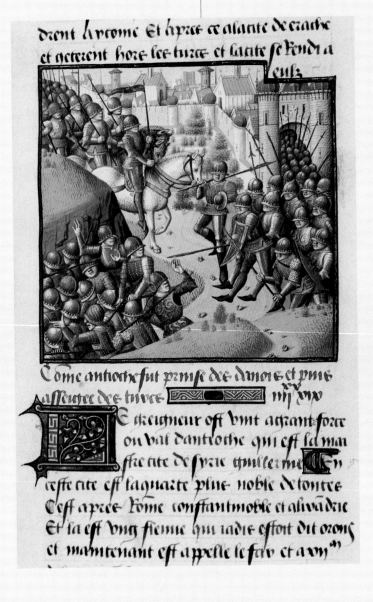

What was to become a persistent problem for the Europeans in the East made its first major appearance here: disease. Before too much time could be spent arguing over what would eventually happen to Antioch, there was an outbreak of plague or typhoid. It killed the one figure of sufficient seniority and wisdom who might have bridged the problems with Alexius: Adhemar of Monteil, the bishop of Le Puy, Urban's representative. The loss of the pope's guiding hand was a subtle blow to the stability of the leadership of the expedition at this point. Each leader was motivated by personal ambition, and the absence of an overall military commander from the West, the recent loosening of bonds with the Byzantines, and the loss of the Church's nominal leader of the campaign allowed these ambitions to manifest themselves, crucially when these territories were captured.

◀ The bishop of Le Puy riding into battle with the Crusader army. He later died at Antioch.

The history of the Latin Kingdoms of the East (as these city states were later referred to) is ultimately one of divide and rule. It has never been resolved whether a single political force backed by a religious consensus could have held these territories more effectively, yet the possibility obviously existed. As it was, any sorrow over the loss of such an able man as Adhemar was felt more by the rank-and-file than among the leadership which, after Baldwin's capture of Edessa and Bohemond's move on Antioch, were out for what they could get.

▼ The wooden siege towers of Raymond of Toulouse are prepared for use in the siege of Antioch.

Celebration eventually gave way to the realization that the job wasn't yet finished. In November, 1098, the army set off again, with their sights on the even greater treasure of Jerusalem. They moved southward, parallel to the

Levantine coast, taking the fortified town of Maarat. In the process, tensions between Bohemond and Raymond flared up—perhaps Bohemond's attempt to take Antioch rankled with the other commander. After the town was seized, and despite his promise to accompany the army to Jerusalem, in return for which Raymond had agreed that he could have Antioch, Bohemond stormed back to his new city to the north. Representatives of the army pressed Raymond to accept overall leadership. The other nobles had their doubts assuaged by payment. Maarat was left to burn as the army marched south, with Raymond in command.

Ironically, by the time they arrived at Jerusalem they found that a change of ownership had taken place. The Fatamids, taking advantage of the Turkish problems with the Christians in the north, had come out of Egypt in force and had retaken the city from the Turks not long after the Crusaders had taken Antioch. Local Arab leaders in this border area between Fatamids, Turks, and Christians were not entirely convinced that these conflicts were such a bad thing. If they managed to tread a fine line of diplomacy between all sides, and kept clear of the fighting, there was considerable autonomy to be gained while their nominal rulers were preoccupied with each other. The Fatamids, who had watched with equanimity as this conflict escalated between their enemies within the faith and the Christians, would soon find themselves in a difficult situation.

▼ Krak des Chevaliers, the Syrian stronghold of the Knights Hospitaler. It contains the remains of Hosn al-Akrad, a Muslim fortress captured by Tancred in 1110.

The change of rule in Jerusalem made no difference to the Crusaders. By the beginning of February they had taken the castle of Hosn al-Akrad. The port of Tortosa was next to fall. After an unsuccessful siege of Arqa, the army moved west to follow the coast southward, anxious to ensure their access to supplies that were coming in on ships owned by Italian merchants. Now that the reputation of the Crusaders had spread, local governors of cities such as Tripoli and Beirut were content to pay them off rather than see their cities ravaged and burned in the cause of defending the rights of ownership of their absent rulers, Turkish or Fatamid. Where there was a possibility of resistance the Crusaders were increasingly keen to pass by, intent on Jerusalem itself. Tyre did not pay, nor was it attacked as they passed. Acre paid. The inhabitants of Ramleh simply fled, leaving a ghost town. Ever southward the Crusaders marched, the common soldiers marveling as they passed more and more places that had previously been known to them only from tales from the Bible. Finally, in June, 1099, they reached Jerusalem.

As forbidding as Jerusalem's fortifications seemed, victory there proved to be more straightforward than at Antioch, despite many indications to the contrary. The Muslim leadership in Jerusalem had driven Christians of all denominations from the city and had substantial supplies that would see them through a lengthy siege. Morale was good since they had heard that the Fatamids were sending an army out of Egypt to destroy these foreign invaders. Yet the Crusaders now had access to the coast and, through that, to Europe, via ships from Genoa and England. They had the confidence gained as a result of their earlier victories and the experience of Antioch, and their final objective was in sight. Though they struggled in the unbearable summer heat of the Holy Land and were debilitated by disease, and though small skirmishes with Muslim forces dogged

▶ The Crusader victory at Bethlehem, June 6th, 1098.

them and disagreements within the Christian camp held them back, there was, they felt, an inevitability about their victory here.

The visions of priests that had played a part since Antioch continued. It was believed that saints were directing action to take place on a particular day, in a particular manner. As the Crusaders liberated legendary places such as Bethlehem with so little effort they must have been overcome with a sense of destiny. There must also have been a sense among the common soldiers that after this they could perhaps go home, and there receive a reception fit for true heroes, true soldiers of Christ.

▲ Godfrey of Bouillon, together with his knights, enters the holy city of Jerusalem.

So it was that, within a couple of weeks, the siege towers had been raised and the Crusaders were attempting to break into the Holy City itself. On July 15th they succeeded. The competition to be the first inside was fierce. Soon soldiers were pouring into the city in great waves and Jerusalem swiftly capitulated. Raymond, as the senior commander, accepted the surrender of the Islamic governor, Iftikhar, there and then ransoming his life and the lives of those he chose to take with him. They were among the few to survive. The army hacked and slaughtered with an evangelical fanaticism. Even a lord as exalted as Tancred, who had guaranteed the safety of a group of Muslims hiding in a mosque, could not protect them from the fury of the soldiers. All were slain, including the Jews who had been allowed to stay—they were viewed as collaborators. Men, women, and children were put to the sword and many were tortured beforehand. For the Jews, news of this barbarity echoed the anti-Semitic attacks that had taken place in Germany at the beginning of the Crusaders' journey. For the Islamic world the monstrous deeds of the Europeans here were something that would never be forgotten. Whatever deals were done after this with local emirs or governors, who had little love for either the Fatamids or the Turks, the acts that took place in Jerusalem that day would always be at the back of their minds.

After much debate, as had occurred in Antioch, Godfrey of Bouillon, Duke of Lower Lorraine, was elected Defender of the Holy Sepulcher. It might perhaps have struck the Crusaders that a churchman would have been more appropriate. Adhemar of Le Puy was dead, however,

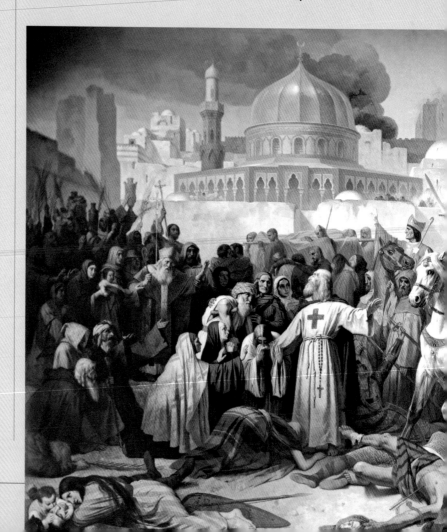

as was the leading Greek contender, Symeon, the exiled patriarch of Jerusalem. Although he was the most senior, Raymond, through his frequent attempts to assume leadership, had turned most of the other nobles against him. Godfrey was seen generally as a pious man and his assumption of the title of defender rather than king both confirmed his piety and defused the tensions that might have arisen at the presumption of kingship in the city of Christ. Once this appointment was made, and the corpses had been removed from the city, news of the long-expected force from the dispossessed Fatamids reached the Christians' ears—but they were obviously too late. This mighty army, led by the Fatamid vizier, Al-Afdal, was taken by surprise outside Ascalon on the way to relieve Jerusalem, and was slaugh-

◄ Having successfully campaigned to take Jerusalem, Godfrey of Bouillon, Duke of Lower Lorraine, was a popular choice as leader of the holy city.

▲ Treasure taken from the vanquished Muslim army is deposited at the Church of the Holy Sepulcher, with Godfrey of Bouillon presiding.

tered. Al-Afdal escaped, retreating to Egypt with a handful of men. The rest were scattered or killed, driven into the desert or into the sea. Much treasure was taken from the vanquished Muslim army and divided among the Christians. The Muslims of Ascalon looked on in horror at the scene that unfolded before them, doubtful of surviving a Crusader attack and terrified, after Jerusalem, by what might become of them should they surrender.

The Crusaders returned to Jerusalem and the scale of their achievement began to sink in. With the realization that they had achieved what they had set out to do, popular feeling began to manifest itself. Many now wanted to return home because their crusading vow to liberate Jerusalem had been fulfilled. Many, however, wanted to stay, particularly those who had set out with the intention of making their names and fortunes in the legendary East. Robert of Normandy and Robert of Flanders gathered together their forces and began to set out for the journey back home. An unhappy Raymond accompanied them. He still held on to a dream of founding his own kingdom and could see little chance of realizing that dream in the south, with Godfrey secure in Jerusalem.

As they headed north along the coast, they reached the Byzantine port of Lattakieh, near Antioch. On their arrival they were alarmed to find that it was under attack from Bohemond, who was acutely aware, having kept Antioch for himself, that he was not in the emperor's favor and was thus keen to secure a port to service the needs of his city. He was being assisted by Daimbert, the archbishop of Pisa. After what must have been a spectacular display of anger by the three nobles, Daimbert called off the blockading ships and, without his support, Bohemond could do little but comply.

The two Roberts returned to Europe via Constantinople to a heroes' welcome. Raymond, having firmly nailed his colors to the Byzantine mast, stayed on in Lattakieh, working out his next move.

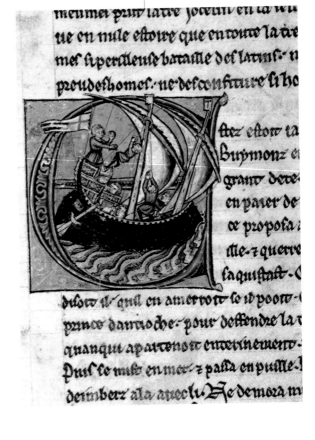

▼ Bohemond of Antioch, accompanied by Archbishop Daimbert of Pisa, sets sail for Apulia in southeastern Italy.

▶ Godfrey formed alliances with the Emirs in order to strengthen his position. Here, he accepts tributes from the Emirs of Caesarea, Ptolemias, and Ascalon.

The promises they had all made on taking up the cross now became pressing. Bohemond of Antioch and Baldwin of Edessa made their pilgrimage to Jerusalem. Godfrey, after the departure of so many men with the armies returning home, was keen to bolster his remaining small force in order to defend the lands in the south. Many of the knights who accompanied Bohemond and Baldwin were induced to stay by the offer of lands and titles. Tancred, meanwhile, had been directing a series of successful raids in Galilee, consolidating the territories held by the Westerners.

With each town taken and each fortress claimed from the Muslims, the position of the Crusaders became more secure. Local Turkish emirs began to make peace with Godfrey. Little was heard from the defeated Fatamids. Alexius, despite the various problems along the way, must have been relieved. At the very least the pressure had been removed from Constantinople. He now had the Crusaders and their military gains as a buffer against the Muslims.

▶ Godfrey of Bouillon is elected Defender of the Holy Sepulcher, leader of the city of Jerusalem.

3 After the First Crusade: The Latin Kingdoms of the East

THE AFTERMATH OF THE FIRST CRUSADE WAS A TIME OF CONSOLIDATION FOR THE VICTORS, EAGER TO TAKE ADVANTAGE OF THE WEALTH AND OTHER BENEFITS OF GAINING TERRITORIES IN THE FAMOUSLY RICH EAST.

Introduction

News of the success of the Crusade had now penetrated Europe, and the first to appear in response had been the representatives of the prosperous Italian maritime states. The wealth of their cities was based exclusively on the trade that came from their fleets, and the goods that they could then sell on into Europe. While they had been able to do business with Islam, they swiftly recognized the new business opportunities that would come with their coreligionists in charge. The Crusaders would not be able to survive without support from Europe. The Venetians were swiftly on the scene, offering the use of their ships and men in further battles in return for preferential treatment and bases in the Holy Land.

After the debacle at Lattakieh, Daimbert arrived in Jerusalem, keen to make both his mark and his fortune. He assumed the role of patriarch, guaranteeing that the Church there would be firmly under the yoke of Rome rather than Constantinople. Then Godfrey was struck down with a disease that would eventually prove fatal. Loyalties were split along family lines on the question of succession. Tancred supported his uncle Bohemond, while Baldwin justified his claim through fraternal ties. Raymond—who had as much claim to leadership of the campaign as any—had failed to make any territory his own and, after Lattakieh, had put himself out of contention by returning to Constantinople to make the most of his relationship with the emperor. While Bohemond's claim was strong, he managed to rule himself out after being captured by the Turks in a conflict in the north and imprisoned

in a remote mountain castle in Asia Minor. Initially Daimbert allied himself with Tancred, but quickly came to accept the realities of the situation. Baldwin, after winning much popular support from Bohemond's army when he interceded to ensure Antioch's protection after their ruler's capture, rode into Jerusalem and was proclaimed king on November 11th, 1100. Daimbert conducted the official coronation ceremony that followed.

▼ The funeral of Godfrey of Bouillon in Jerusalem, July 23rd, 1100. His passing deprived Jerusalem of a capable leader.

BAVDOVIN·FONDE·L'EMPIRE· LATIN·DE·CôSTANTINOPLE·

▲ Baldwin I of Boulogne, Count of Edessa, and brother of Godfrey of Bouillon, was declared King of Jerusalem on November 11th, 1100.

Baldwin's reign

Baldwin proved to be a fortunate and exemplary choice. He recognized that the key to holding on to the conquests was solidarity among the leaders of the Crusade and the establishment of defendable kingdoms. Throughout his reign he proved his talents as a leader time and again by his subtle and skilled negotiations with both allies and enemies. The two senior leaders, Bohemond and Raymond, were, in one way or another, sidelined. The others never seriously challenged Baldwin's position as overlord.

The political state of the area at the opening of the twelfth century was complex. Alexius had won back much of western Asia Minor and many of the coastal areas of the south through his own skillful maneuverings and by taking advantage of the fact that many of his opponents were preoccupied with the Franks. (Franks was a term used by the Muslims to describe all the newcomers from Europe.) To his east were his old Muslim enemies, the Seljuks of Rum, who were now as concerned with their neighboring fellow Muslims, the Danishmends, the Norman-controlled principality of Antioch, and, to a lesser extent, the county of Edessa, as they were with the emperor. Edessa itself was in an unenviable position. With the exception of the Normans to the west, who were never the most reliable of allies, it was surrounded on every other side by Muslim forces: Rum to the northwest, the Danishmends to the north, the Ortoqids to the east, and several semi-independent Muslim rulers to the south. It was a territory that was impossible to defend adequately: it was only the fortresses of Edessa that were held, not the countryside. Edessa was also, to a great extent, Armenian, and the Armenian people were less comfortable with foreign rule than the melting-pot communities of the coast. It lacked the riches of a great city such as Antioch and the mercantile opportunities of the ports, and, with an impoverished peasantry who scratched a poor living from the land when they were not being put to the sword by invaders, there was little chance of generating great revenue through taxes. Baldwin's cousin and the man who was to inherit Edessa from him, another Baldwin, this time originally of Le Bourg, became notorious for raising a substantial sum to pay his army by blackmailing his father-in-law, Gabriel. Local custom dictated that men wore beards—when Baldwin threatened to shave his father-in-law's, Gabriel handed over 30,000 bezants to avoid the shame this would bring on the family.

Between these two Christian states and the kingdom of Jerusalem lay independent Islamic cities, whose loyalties had traditionally been obtained by force, either by the Fatamids of Egypt or the Abbasids of the Middle East, and bandit territory. Baldwin had three strategic

◀ Baldwin had proved to be a popular leader, and the citizens of Edessa turned out in force to pay homage at his funeral.

aims: to protect his northern borders by removing the intervening Muslim rulers between the Latin lands; to protect his western flank by control of the coastal cities of the Levant, hence guaranteeing supplies of materials and men arriving from Europe; and to extend the southern borders until he reached the Red Sea, preventing the Fatamids from providing easy support to other Muslims. By the time of his death in 1119, Baldwin had achieved each of these aims. He almost lost his life several times in confrontations with the enemy, sometimes escaping death narrowly. He fought enemies within as well as without. Daimbert's greed saw him exiled twice, the second time for good. Each battle won, each city successfully besieged made the long-term survival of the Latin Kingdom of Jerusalem more likely.

▲ Mixing between the different groups inevitably brought Crusaders and Saracens into social contact. Here, Christian and Muslim face each other in amicable combat across a chessboard.

Within the kingdom Baldwin encouraged mixing between the different groups, to the extent of allowing marriage between Christians and Muslims. Most importantly, in terms of conflict, he withstood the forces of Fatamid Egypt. Their defeat for the third time at Ramleh appeared to be final. Against Baldwin's greatness, the others often seemed like bit-players in an enormous farce.

To win Tancred over to the idea of Baldwin's kingship, the latter had found it necessary to offer his rival the position of regent of Antioch, a role that was then to be relinquished when Bohemond was released. After objecting vehemently to the short-term nature of this appointment, Tancred eventually realized that this position might not turn out to be so temporary after all. This removed the most troublesome of Baldwin's allies to a convenient distance and yet it made use of

◄ A tournament pitches Crusaders and Saracens against each other in the type of friendly match that was part of Baldwin's policy of integration.

him—Tancred was as able as he was difficult and before Bohemond's capture he had adroitly taken much of Galilee to the north of Jerusalem. Giving him Antioch was both a reward and a burden. Relations between the Byzantines and the Normans had been difficult since long before the Crusades. The Normans had taken Byzantine land in southern Italy; they had fought against the empire in Greece. It was no accident that a previous emperor had chosen to replace his personal bodyguard of Normans with one made up of Anglo-Saxon exiles who had fled England after William the Conqueror had taken control. Alexius would never forgive Bohemond for his refusal to relinquish Antioch—encouraging the persistence of enmity between the two by ensuring that Antioch remained out of the former's hands might have seemed advantageous to a king of Jerusalem who could have expected interference from both.

In 1101 more Crusaders set out from Europe, heartened by the success of the First Crusade and keen to play a part. Some were old hands. Stephen of Blois was among them, perhaps keen to make up for his flight from the siege of Antioch. At Constantinople they met both the emperor and Raymond. In all, three such armies came into Asia Minor and each was annihilated in turn by the Turks, whose self-confidence increased with every calamity inflicted. For Raymond, who had joined them from Constantinople, the disaster that overcame each army must have been close to the final straw. However, nothing prepared him for the reception that he was to receive when he arrived at Antioch with the other surviving nobility from the new campaigns. The grand welcome extended even to the "cowardly" Stephen of Blois vanished when Raymond appeared. Tancred's lieutenant, Bernard the Stranger,

▼ Tancred takes the city of Tarsus in September 1097.

◀ A group of Knights of the Holy Spirit set out for the Holy Land in 1101, enthusiastic about playing their part in the Crusade.

stepped forward and arrested him, ostensibly on account of his behavior in one of these later disasters of the Crusade. There was popular indignation over the arrest, but Tancred managed to persuade Raymond to swear an oath to the effect that he would abandon any interest in that area. Raymond was set free, and promptly left with a force in a southerly direction.

Tancred then turned to the task that had defeated his uncle—the capture of the port of Lattakieh. He succeeded after a long siege. Alexius was furious. Tancred was not the most popular of figures

▼ The port of Lattakieh in Syria, captured by Tancred and later recovered by Alexius.

and, ironically, as an inevitable consequence of his success, an international ransom was collected to free Bohemond. When Bohemond was finally released in 1103, Tancred was one of the few who hadn't offered to contribute to the fund. Bohemond thanked him for his stewardship of Antioch and assumed rule of the city. It was fortunate for Tancred that very soon afterward, Baldwin II was captured and Tancred was able to step neatly into his shoes, again on the basis that it was a temporary position. The response of Baldwin II, whose growing distrust of Tancred had led him to be one of the prime instigators of the ransoming of Bohemond, could not have been positive. He must have wondered who would be likely to ransom him. When an opportunity arrived in the shape of a Seljuk princess captured by Tancred, the offer of an exchange of Baldwin for the Seljuk by the Turks—an act strongly encouraged by Baldwin of Jerusalem—was

quietly turned down, the two Norman leaders opting for hard currency rather than a ransomed noble.

With increased Turkish pressure on Antioch, Alexius decided it was time to take action and launched a successful recovery of much of Lattakieh. Bohemond realized that he was in an increasingly difficult situation. The only support he could envisage would be from Europe, so he set off to Rome to convince Urban II's successor, Paschal, that the Byzantines were a greater threat than the Turks. With papal backing he launched an attack on the empire, an act that poisoned for ever the relationship between the two divisions of the Church. He was eventually defeated by Alexius, humiliated by having to swear fealty to him, and retired to his provinces in Italy. He died there, never having returned to Antioch, which was now held, as was Edessa, by Tancred.

▲ Bertrand de Saint-Gilles, "Bertrand the Bastard," receives homage from a Muslim ruler.

After being exiled from Antioch, Raymond persisted with his plans to acquire his own little kingdom. He succeeded in taking Tortosa on the Levantine coast and he won some spectacular battles against the Muslims. A hero to his own troops, he died some months after receiving burns in an unsuccessful siege of Tripoli, having gone some way toward restoring his dignity. His followers there elected his cousin, William-Jordan of Cerdagne, as his successor, an inheritance that was disputed when Raymond's illegitimate son, Bertrand the Bastard, turned up from France. As the two men went about capturing towns and cities in the Levant ill-feeling intensified between them. William-Jordan sought Tancred's support while Bertrand looked to Baldwin. Things reached a head and Baldwin was forced to divide the conquered land between William-Jordan and Bertrand, to be unified under whoever outlived the other. When William-Jordan, in the security of his own camp, met an unexplained death not long afterward, a new county of Tripoli, perched on the coast between Antioch and Jerusalem, was created and joined the other three kingdoms.

By now Baldwin II had been ransomed and, after a struggle, had persuaded Tancred to return Edessa to him. The enmity between Baldwin and Tancred is best illustrated by the battle between the Muslim forces of Jawali and Ridwan in 1108. Tancred and Baldwin both participated—on opposing sides. Later, at the same conference that had been called to sort out the differences between William-Jordan and Bertrand, Baldwin of Jerusalem had to take action to reconcile Tancred and Baldwin II.

By 1111, Alexius in turn had had his fill of Tancred. He sent his envoys to the east to meet with the caliph of Baghdad in an attempt to convince him to move on Tancred's principality. Alexius' men were not the first to come to Baghdad with this suggestion. When they arrived they found Muslims from Aleppo urging the same course of action. When the purpose of Alexius' mission was made known, he heard that the rabble had proclaimed him a greater Muslim than the unwilling caliph.

▼ The leader of the Assassins, the Old Man of the Mountains, chooses three young men as recruits to the cult, giving them an intoxicating elixir.

A new force entered Muslim politics at this time, a cult organized by a man known as Hassan-I-Sabah. In time each leader of this cult, the Assassins, became known as the Old Man of the Mountains. The Assassins were members of an Ismaili sect who directed their energies, as a consequence of their religious beliefs, against their fellow-Muslims the Abbasids in the East, and their masters there, the Seljuk Turks, a

▲ Baldwin of Jerusalem on his deathbed, surrounded by Crusaders and churchmen.

separate dynasty from the Seljuks in Asia Minor. All Sunni Muslims had learned to fear the Assassins and the Crusaders soon did likewise. The adherents of the cult were anonymous, rumored to be on drugs, and cared little for their earthly fate once their victims had been despatched. Their reputation was more effective than their acts. The ever-present fear of a sudden attack in the middle of a crowded marketplace or square served to raise paranoia levels among leaders.

At this stage a generation of Crusaders began to pass away. Tancred was taken by disease in 1112. Alexius died in 1118. The following year saw the death of Baldwin of Jerusalem. He had almost become a legend by this time, the most popular leader among the Latins in the Holy Land. The throne passed to his cousin, Baldwin of Edessa. Almost immediately Baldwin's mettle was tested in an attempt against the Franks by the Ortoqids. The Crusaders lost men in a number of battles, suffering particularly when most of the army of Antioch was massacred at what became known as the Field of Blood, but Baldwin managed to steer them through these troubles with most of their territories left intact, thus confirming his primacy among the rulers of the Latin Kingdoms.

Support from Europe now came in a different form. In the years before the First Crusade an order known as the Hospitalers had been formed to support pilgrims on their way to the Holy Land. Soon after Baldwin's rise the idea arose to turn this order into something more. Moving from passive support to an active role, the Hospitalers became a military order, an organization of knights dedicated to ensuring the continued success of the Crusades. At the same time, another order, that of the Knights of the Temple, the Templars, was created. The idea spread. In the coming decades more and more orders were formed, in the Holy Land and in Europe, combining religious dedication and knightly valor. None were to prove as successful, or in the end as wealthy, as the Hospitalers and the Templars. Although the numbers of knights they provided for action in the East were never huge, they would often provide an invaluable additional and self-financing force. They were also to prove an almost unparalleled source of dissension in the latter years of the Latin Kingdoms.

▼ Pilgrims arrive outside the city of Jerusalem, escorted by a group of Knights Templar.

◄ The Fortress of St. Gilles, Tripoli, Lebanon, built in 1109 by Raymond of St. Gilles, Count of Toulouse, and renovated in the fourteenth and sixteenth centuries.

Control of Edessa passed to Joscelin of Courtenay, a relative of Baldwin. The Franks, after the successful resistance against the Ortoqids, were soon in difficulty again. Joscelin was captured in 1123 and before long Baldwin himself had joined him. An undercover force of Armenians rescued them from prison before the Muslims could make anything of holding two of the three most senior Christian rulers in the region.

The Venetians were brought in with an attempt to take Tyre, an island fortress that Alexander the Great had joined to the coast by a strip of land when he captured it more than a thousand years earlier. After a long siege it fell, the first important gain made by the Christians in

► The count of Tripoli accepts the surrender of the city of Tyre in 1124.

many years. Bohemond's young son, Bohemond II, came out from Italy to claim his principality of Antioch. The handsome and promising youth's career was to be cut short—by 1130 his severed head was an embalmed gift in the palace of the caliph of Baghdad. The final members of the old guard passed with the long, lingering death of Baldwin II in 1131 and the death of Joscelin of Edessa in the same year from wounds sustained during a siege when one of his own tunnels collapsed under him.

The Latin Kingdoms of the East had endured for 30 years. Despite the potentially overwhelming forces surrounding them, a strong and generally unified leadership had enabled them to hold firm against

opponents who were usually in disarray. Attachments to the West were still strong—more and more pilgrims were making the journey to the East. Trade was facilitated through the capture of more coastal towns and closer links with Genoa and Venice, though the deals struck with the two Italian city states began to result in more and more of the profits that might have bolstered the East passing into Italian hands. The military orders were bringing additional fighting power and strengthening the connections with Europe: the Assassins had divided the Muslims further.

The forces of Islam needed a leader they could stand behind, a heroic figure who could unite them. The first step was to realize that their true enemies were not each other. The pendulum was to swing back toward Islam over the next few years. The Crusaders had already reached their peak in some respects, although they did not recognize it at the time. The novelty of the appeal of the original Crusade became difficult to re-create. Winning back Jerusalem was an easier concept to sell to the West than retaining a hold on it and, as it gradually became apparent that the support of Europe was to be a constant requirement, the new Latin rulers of the East must have wondered for how long that support could be relied upon.

◀ Tyre is captured by the Venetians in 1123 under the leadership of Doge Domenico Michiel.

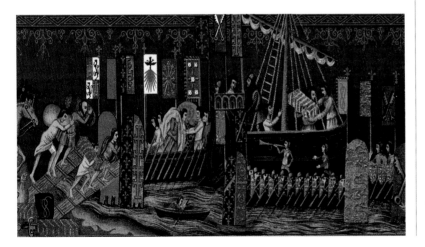

◀ A company of crusading Knights of the Holy Spirit prepare to set sail for Palestine.

4 The Second Crusade

WHEN NEWS CAME IN 1145 THAT EDESSA HAD BEEN RECAPTURED BY MUSLIMS, THE TIME SEEMED RIPE FOR A SECOND CRUSADE. CALLED TO ARMS BY POPE EUGENIUS III AND ST. BERNARD OF CLAIRVAUX, A HUGE FORCE SET OUT IN 1145 TO LIBERATE THE HOLY LAND ONCE AGAIN.

Introduction

For the Latin Kingdoms, the Second Crusade should have been a marvelous boost. By 1145, news reached the pope, Eugenius III, that the county of Edessa had fallen. After almost 50 years the joyous news of the First Crusade had settled down into a comfortable acceptance of Christianity's preeminence in the Holy Land. Church bells had rung throughout Europe's countryside at the news of Jerusalem's recapture. The reports of the retaking of Edessa by the Muslims was used by Eugenius to issue a new call to arms, and this caught the imagination of many of the nobility of Western Europe. There was, once again, the chance for younger sons passed over in succession to win lands in the Levant, the opportunity to match the heroic deeds of fathers, uncles, grandfathers, or great uncles who had gone across the Mediterranean to fight in that most laudable of contests.

Eugenius chose King Louis VII of France as leader of the Crusade. The problems associated with a split leadership were lessons that had been learnt. What Eugenius did not count on was the enthusiasm of St. Bernard of Clairvaux, the preeminent churchman of the time, who, having been delegated by the pope to preach the Crusade in France, carried the call into Germany,

▲ King Louis VII of France receives the pilgrim's staff from Eugenius III in acknowledgment of his role as leader of the Second Crusade.

infecting King Conrad with his enthusiasm. Two huge armies set off in 1147 under the two kings. Conrad was the first to arrive in Constantinople, having trailed chaos in the wake of his army on the way. Louis followed soon afterward. Tensions between the French and Germans were strong.

A useful ally could have been King Roger II of Sicily, a Norman lord who, in addition to Sicily, owned much of southern Italy. Roger had experience in fighting the Muslims, having taken Malta and, after several attempts, Tripoli, establishing a Norman colony on the North African coast. He also had a substantial sea force. Unfortunately, Roger had ruffled a lot of feathers by his claims to Antioch—as Bohemond's nearest male heir—and to Jerusalem, on foot of his mother's marriage to Baldwin I (where a contract had been signed promising him the succession). Eugenius had fallen out with Roger, so the benefits of a third army were lost.

A new campaign

Conrad's army left for Asia Minor. Ignoring the suggestion of the Byzantine emperor, Manuel, that they travel as far as possible through his territory on the way to the Holy Land, the over-confident Germans set off straight into Seljuk country. They did not have sufficient supplies for the journey, and were certainly not prepared for the reception they received. Overcome with thirst, they broke formation to obtain water at the first opportunity. The knights climbed down from their horses and, without any semblance of order, stumbled toward the river before them. The waiting Turks descended upon them and a tremendous slaughter ensued. Conrad survived with a fragment of the army, and fled back toward Byzantine territory. When news of the Germans' fate reached Louis he decided to take Manuel's earlier advice. His army traveled by land until they arrived at a convenient point where Louis and most of the nobility could take to the sea. The unfortunate remainder of his force, along with the remnants of the hapless German army, finally reached Antioch after almost constant harrying by the Turks along the way. Despite attempts to convince him to fight there, Louis decided to proceed to Jerusalem.

He arrived to find that Conrad, who had initially stayed in Constantinople to recuperate, had got there before him—sensibly traveling by sea from Manuel's capital direct to Acre. By now Manuel's reputation among the new Crusaders was in shreds. As their predecessors had before, these Crusaders blamed the Byzantines for everything that had gone wrong. The final straw was Manuel's treaty

▼ Louis VII of France and Conrad III of Germany enter the city of Constantinople together.

▲ Louis VII, Conrad III, and Baldwin III meet to plan the siege of Damascus.

with the Seljuk Turks of Asia Minor, the same forces who had slaughtered so many of their fellow countrymen. The fact that he was forced into it, urgently needing to free up his forces to fight in Greece against Roger of Sicily (who had taken the opportunity of the distractions in Asia Minor to invade) was of no concern to them. This act of diplomacy confirmed the prejudices of the Westerners.

The arrival in Jerusalem, however, was a cause for celebration among the inhabitants. Queen Melisende, daughter of Baldwin II, had ruled the city jointly with her teenage son, Baldwin III, since the death of her husband, Fulk of Anjou, in 1143. Thoughts of reconquering Edessa fell by the wayside. It was decided instead to launch an attack on the nearest rich Muslim capital, Damascus. This was not to prove the wisest of moves.

▲ The army of Crusaders come together under Baldwin at the River Barada outside Damascus.

One candidate for the role of the heroic figurehead that Islam had been waiting for had appeared a few decades earlier. Imad ad-din Zangi ibn aq Sonqur, commonly referred to as Zangi, was the son of the governor of Aleppo. Through skillful maneuvering, and the support of the Seljuks, he extended his control from Mosul to an ever-increasing area of Syria. It was Zangi who had conquered Edessa—an act that had catapulted him to fame in the Islamic world. He saw himself as the man to rid Islam of the Franks and, when not fighting them directly, took on those Muslims who chose to ally themselves with the Christians. The success of Edessa was never followed up. Zangi had wanted to press on and take control of Damascus—had he succeeded he would have been a perpetual thorn in side of the Latin Kingdoms. However, it was not to be. In 1146 a eunuch murdered him in his sleep, in the middle of a campaign to lay siege to the stronghold of a rebellious Arab prince.

The Franks must have breathed a sigh of collective relief. Their joy was short-lived, however. Zangi's son, Nur ed-Din, stepped into his shoes and proved to be made of the same sort of stuff as his father, with the same intent—to send the Franks, those that he did not put to the sword, hurrying back to Europe. Nur ed-Din had also inherited his father's ambition to take Damascus, a town ruled by the Emir Unur. Unur, eager to remain independent, was in a difficult position.

◀ The city of Damascus today.

Caught between the Franks and Nur ed-Din he cultivated a good relationship with the former, suspecting that they represented less of a threat to him.

When the mighty combined force of Louis and Conrad and the Latin Kingdoms appeared outside Damascus, its soldiers confidently walking in the city's orchards and through the gardens on the outskirts, Unur was faced with a terrible decision. Should he call for help from Nur ed-Din? While he could he drew in local reinforcements and fortified the city. A few skirmishes took place, with the Franks making more than their fair share of mistakes. However, it soon became clear that, in the end, Unur would not be able to resist their tremendous advantage of numbers. Forced by circumstance, he entered into discussions with Nur ed-Din. When news of these talks reached the ears of the Latins, the folly of what they had embarked on became clear. News of the army being gathered by Nur ed-Din began to come through. While the Franks were confident of their ability to take Damascus on its own, Nur ed-Din's entry into the fray not only jeopardized the possibility of their taking the city but also increased the risk of a complete defeat by the hostile and powerful enemy that was establishing itself right on their borders. Or so the threat appeared to the native, Christian nobles. Louis and Conrad, on the other hand, couldn't see that there was a problem. Muslims were Muslims—so why the sudden change of heart? As time went on, the Latins' nerves failed. They convinced Louis and Conrad to retreat. Damascus was safe from both for the time being, and the Second Crusade was effectively over.

▼ The siege of Damascus—Baldwin, Conrad, and Louis of France take their place at the head of their troops. The Crusaders retreated after four days.

Conrad returned to Europe. Any responsibility for the failure of the Crusade that might have been attributed to Constantinople was forgotten. His hatred of Roger of Sicily was paramount, and any foe of Roger's was a friend of his. Louis remained in the East for a while, uncertain about what he should do. Eventually he too returned to Europe. Louis laid the blame for the failure of the Crusade firmly at Manuel's door. Once back in France he agitated against Manuel but, without Conrad's support, a new crusade, this time against Constantinople, was out of the question, however much the Roman Church might have supported it. Neither Conrad nor Louis can have had great respect for the leaders of Outremer after the debacle at Damascus. The new Crusaders had been shocked by what they found in the East: Westerners adopting Eastern dress and fraternizing with Infidels. Naively, they had expected a society similar to the one they knew in Europe. What they found was a melting-pot of West and East, a society where merchants from Genoa and Venice mixed with their Arab counterparts, a place where the members of numerous heretical Christian cults lived alongside adherents of the true faith of Rome. In 50 years generations had grown up in the East whose idea of Europe was based on what they heard from pilgrims, and on the tales told by their parents and grandparents. The new Crusaders were laboring under a huge misapprehension. They had come to take part in a holy war but, as far as the people they were trying to save were concerned, it was an almost entirely political affair.

As a consequence, the Latin Kingdoms would have to wait years before more help would be forthcoming from Europe. Nur ed-Din would consolidate his power. And a man would soon come who would assume an even more heroic role in Islamic eyes, the greatest figure to take the field against the foreign invaders—Saladin.

▼ Louis and Conrad leave the Holy Land together in the wake of the retreat from Damascus.

◄ Pilgrims to the Holy Land arrive at the port of Jaffa. These travelers were the only source of news from Europe for the Christians of the East.

5 Background to the Third Crusade

FOLLOWING THE FAILURE OF THE SECOND CRUSADE, MUSLIM AND CHRISTIAN RULERS ALIKE STROVE TO CONSOLIDATE THEIR POSITIONS. AT ONE POINT, BOTH SIDES WERE LEADERLESS, AND WHILE THE CHRISTIANS ENGAGED IN FACTION FIGHTING, A NEW MUSLIM LEADER—SALADIN—WAS MAKING HIS PRESENCE FELT.

Introduction

In the years following the Second Crusade, Nur ed-Din strengthened his grip on the lands surrounding the Christians. The success was not entirely one-sided. King Baldwin III, now ruling alone, took the great southern coastal fortress of Ascalon in 1153. This was a prestigious victory and bolstered Outremer's defenses against a possible attack from the Fatamid regime in Egypt, though the Fatamid threat had actually reduced with the passage of time after a succession of weak rulers. What was an entirely more pertinent yet quieter victory came the following year when the populace of Damascus received Nur ed-Din into their city and their hearts. Nur ed-Din did not press this new advantage over the Christians immediately. Other concerns were soon foremost in his mind. Earthquakes struck the region in 1156 and coping with the ensuing damage occupied Christian and Muslim alike.

▼ The fortress city of Ascalon is handed over to Baldwin III of Jerusalem, August 19th, 1153.

Conflict was now centered on the north. Reynald of Châtillon was another of those sons of the nobility persuaded by the laws of primogeniture to stay on in the East to seek his fortune after Louis of France had left. He decided to take the matrimonial route to power, marrying Constance, the widow of Prince Raymond of Antioch. However, this was not enough for him. Taking advantage of Manuel's preoccupations he made Antioch live up to its reputation as a thorn in the empire's side once again. While Manuel was occupied with the Seljuks and their Armenian neighbors, Reynald combined with the Templars to formulate a plan to raid the rich island of Cyprus, which was under Byzantine control. Though the military orders, through the policing and guarding of pilgrim routes and fortresses, and through their contribution as elite warriors in battle, made a much-needed contribution to preserving the status quo, their independent leadership worked against the greater interests of the Franks. In addition, rivalries between the orders would prove to be very destructive.

▲ King Baldwin III visits the Byzantine emperor Manuel Comnenus in his pavilion.

Reynald, as an outsider in Antioch, was not greatly loved. He arrested and tortured a leading and much respected wealthy churchman of the city, anointed his still-fresh wounds with honey, and then staked him to a roof until the ministrations of the local ants, flies, and wasps convinced him to donate his wealth to the cause. Reynald set out to Cyprus with these funds and, in the process of liberating the island of its wealth and potential hostages, reduced it to a state of such misery that it became the target of any pirate in the area. Baldwin was horrified and Manuel was filled with rage. When Reynald was later captured by Muslims the rejoicing of peasants and nobles alike, could be heard from Constantinople to Jerusalem

A new crusade

In 1162, Baldwin III died at the relatively young age of 33. His brother Amalric, count of Ascalon, took the throne. Meanwhile, weak rule in Egypt caused the kingdom to descend into a state of near-chaos. Nur ed-Din saw an opportunity to conquer both Egypt and Amalric, at the very least, a requirement to ensure that it did not fall into Amalric's hands. After a game of cat-and-mouse, during which Amalric would head south toward the Nile and then be dragged back by Nur ed-Din's attacks in his absence, 1167 saw armies of both sides near Cairo. The Franks were led by Amalric; the Muslims by Nur ed-Din's right-hand man, Shirkuh. With Shirkuh was his nephew, a young man by the name of Saladin. The Egyptians knew that the Franks could be bought off but Nur ed-Din wanted to build an empire. However, with Fatamid money in their purses, the Franks and their Egyptian allies presented too formidable an opponent and Shirkuh eventually withdrew. Amalric, the threat to him removed, and substantially richer, followed.

Rumors of the friendship between Shirkuh and the son of the Egyptian vizier, a desire for more gold, and the interests of new Crusaders from the West soon brought back an army under Amalric. The vizier, Shawar, was horrified. He contacted Shirkuh and, through him, Nur ed-Din. Playing the two sides off against each other in the way that Damascus had, years earlier, was not going to work on this occasion. Nur ed-Din would not make the same mistake again. Shirkuh and Saladin returned to Egypt and, grasping the opportunity presented by fate, met up with the unsuspecting vizier. In a very short time, they had ended his rule of Egypt by beheading him. Shawar had never been very popular, and Shirkuh was sufficiently canny to inveigle his way into the kingship, as the loyal servant of Nur ed-Din. Within months, Shirkuh had died after having celebrated to excess.

Whoever was to blame for the situation, Amalric and his barons were in agreement that they were now in great difficulty. Amalric sent requests for a new crusade to anybody of major standing in Europe that he could think of. However, his contacts were all otherwise engaged, so he turned to the only possible source of aid, Manuel. In 1169, a joint force set off for Egypt—Amalric over land, the Byzantines by sea. Their attempt produced no positive result. The Franks were too cautious to attack, the Byzantines too short of supplies—a situation that was aggravated by the impoverished state of Cyprus—to wait. Recriminations flew between the two sides. In 1170, to add to their problems, earthquakes struck again.

▼ The siege and capture of the city of Tanis during Amalric's Egyptian campaign.

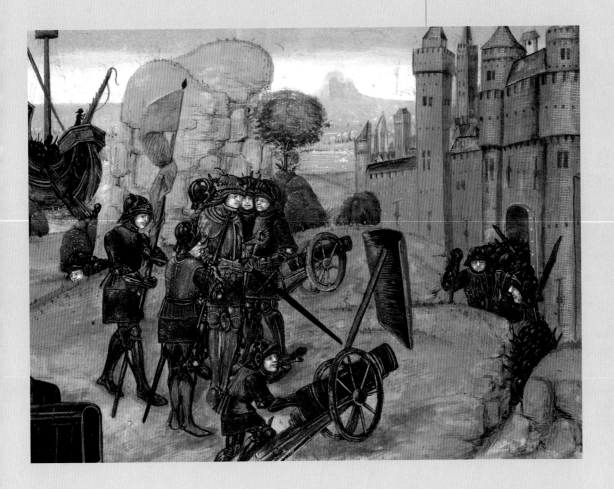

Saladin inherited Egypt from Shirkuh. With Egypt added to his territories, Nur ed-Din should have moved against the Franks. However, he was becoming increasingly distrustful of Saladin. Saladin had his own problems—with potential coups against him at home and the fact that Nur ed-Din was uncertain of his loyalty he was disinclined to take up arms against the Franks. Saladin simply could not ignore the benefits of having a buffer between himself and his master. His excuses were met with increasing suspicion; his apologies and vows of obeisance became less and less convincing. In the end he was saved by Nur ed-Din's death in May, 1174. Any Frankish joy at this event was brought to an end by the death of Amalric two months later.

At first both sides seemed to be in the same position—without a leader. The role that Saladin would later play was not readily apparent at this point. For the Franks the situation was desperate. Amalric's only son, Baldwin, was a 13-year-old leper. There was a lot of dissension among their various factions and the Templars were increasingly following a program that was at odds with the Frankish barons. Amalric had received ambassadors from the Assassins in 1173 suggesting an alliance against Nur ed-Din. The Assassins' leader, Rashid ed-Din Sinan—the preeminent Old Man of the Mountains—was a cunning and dangerous opponent. As an ally he represented, at the very least, a terrorist who could act as a major irritant to the Franks' main enemy. After a very positive meeting, the ambassadors left and were promptly ambushed and slaughtered by a group of Templars. Outraged, Amalric sought to punish the ringleader of the offending knights and had to take him by force when the Templar Grand Master refused to hand him over.

The Templars pursued a far more rigid policy than most of refusing to negotiate with the enemy and, for them, the enemy was every

▼ A contemporary miniature of the Islamic leader Saladin.

◄ Nur ed-Din is defeated
in battle by Hugh le Brun,
Hugh X of Lusignan.

Muslim. In this they found common cause with the new Crusaders, who still provided a small but steady source of fighting men. In opposition were the more pragmatic Knights Hospitaler and most of the local barony. While Amalric was alive and the Templars and recent immigrants were without a figurehead, these tensions were controlled. However, within a year of Amalric's death, the freeing of Reynald of Châtillon provided the latter group with someone who would fill the position of leader. Raymond of Tripoli was by then acting as regent in Jerusalem while the young leper prince, growing increasingly weaker, edged toward his maturity. Neither of them could be expected to impose their will upon dissenters with the same force as the able and experienced Amalric.

In Asia Minor things were also going very badly for the Byzantines. After a period of détente with the Seljuks, tensions were rising. Manuel decided to sort them out once and for all. He sent out an army under his cousin, Andronicus, but it was defeated at Niksar and Andronicus was beheaded. Manuel followed this with an army that displayed the full might of the empire and it, in turn, was crushed mercilessly by the Turks at Myriocephalum in 1176. In Europe and among certain Christian factions there was rejoicing at the defeat of the treacherous Byzantines. As far as the Franks of a less evangelical persuasion were concerned, the removal of the Greeks as a deciding force in Asia Minor simply meant that the Seljuks would soon be free to turn their attentions south.

The next few years saw Saladin gradually tighten the pressure on the Franks. Egypt's natural resources were considerable. It had been the breadbasket of the ancient world and much of the considerable maritime traffic in exotic goods from India and the Far East passed through its ports on the way to Europe. Compared to the Latin Kingdoms it was extremely rich. Without support from Europe things would deteriorate for the Christians. They defeated Saladin at Montgisard in 1177 by drawing on every man they could find and ambushing the Muslims. But the tide had turned after the better part of a century of success for the Franks. Once again, nature interceded on their behalf—this time in the shape of famine. Saladin agreed to a two-year truce with the young leper king in 1180, using the time gained to strengthen his control over his governors and to force peace treaties with the few remaining independent Muslim forces, such as the Seljuks.

Among the Franks, the extremist forces around Reynald gained power at the expense of others. Baldwin, particularly without Raymond as regent, could not stand against them. The few sound advisors he had were either marginalized or deceased. In Constantinople, Manuel

▶ Saladin, Sultan of Egypt during the Second Crusade. His success prompted the pope to call for the Third Crusade.

▶ Although greatly incapacitated by his disease, Baldwin IV fought valiantly with his troops at the Battle of Montgisard in 1177, which resulted in a decisive victory for the kingdom of Jerusalem.

himself was dying and in Jerusalem the young leper king's illness was progressing apace.

After Manuel's death the empire was in upheaval. One ruler followed swiftly after another. Notoriously, in 1182, some of the tensions between vying factions in the palace erupted in a spontaneous attack by the common people on the Westerners living in the capital. Most were killed, and it was a day that would never be forgotten in the West, whatever restitution was made. For the Franks, what aggravated this crime was the existence of a non-aggression pact between the Byzantines and Saladin.

Outside of Egypt, Saladin's empire continued to expand. By 1183 he had moved his capital to Damascus as a more central point from which to rule. In Jerusalem the exercise of power was in the hands

of Baldwin's brother-in-law, Guy. The king's leprosy had advanced to the point where he was bedridden and decaying. Reynald, in a particular stroke of genius, chose this time to set out on a maritime expedition into the Red Sea. Most of his victims there proved to be Muslim pilgrims. More odium was heaped upon the Franks in response and the few friends they had among the Muslims were lost through this act of impiety. Guy and Baldwin fell out with each other and Baldwin reclaimed his role as king for a final few months before his death in 1185. Saladin agreed to another truce, this time for four years, and, as before, used the time to consolidate his power. Baldwin's nephew, Baldwin V, a young child, was appointed king, with Raymond once again declared regent. The child died at the age of nine and Guy and his wife claimed the throne after some dissent. More problems were to come from Reynald, who, having been instrumental in Guy's accession, now felt he could act without constraint. Again, he proceeded to raid Muslim merchant caravans, despite the truce with Saladin.

When Saladin finally made his move it was the greatest calamity to befall Outremer. His army met the combined forces of the Latin Kingdoms, with both Templars and Hospitalers taking part, at Hattin in 1187. The Crusaders were boxed in, desperate for water, while the surrounding Muslims jubilantly anticipated victory. Raymond was heard to cry out, "Ah, Lord God, the war is over; we are dead men;

▶ The Battle of Hattin in 1187 was a decisive victory for Saladin's army, enabling Islam to become the preeminent military power in the Holy Land.

the kingdom is finished," as the parched soldiers lay there through the night, acrid smoke from the bushes surrounding the camp, which had been set alight by the Muslims, adding to their discomfort. The next morning at dawn the Muslims attacked. A tiny force escaped from the mass slaughter. Many of the senior figures were captured and brought to Saladin's tent, King Guy and Reynald and the Grand Master of the Templars among them. Forgiveness was not to the forefront of Saladin's mind.

All of the Templars captured were given over to the Sufi mystics who had followed the army—they took great delight in torturing and then killing them. Reynald, as the most hated figure in the Islamic world, did not even bother pleading for his life. The little he did manage to say before Saladin picked up his sword, walked over to him, and despatched him to the next world, is unrecorded. Even with so many dead, the market was bloated with Frankish prisoners—a slave could be bought for the price of a pair of sandals.

▲ Reynald of Chatillon sits despondently at the feet of a victorious Saladin.

From here the victors went on to capture most of the kingdom of Jerusalem. Soon the territory held by the Franks was restricted to fortresses and the city of Jerusalem itself. Christians from the surrounding countryside flocked to Jerusalem and prayed for God's mercy in their time of trial. In 1187, Jerusalem fell to Saladin. More and more refugees made their way to the coast, hoping for a passage out, aware that the great coastal fortresses like Tyre were their last hope. South of Tripoli, the Franks had almost been swept from the map. The Christian rule of Jerusalem had lasted barely a century. Now it had fallen to the one man who was capable of uniting the Islamic world against the foreign invaders. Could Christian Europe take it back?

6 The Third Crusade

THE THIRD CRUSADE PROVED DIFFICULT TO RAISE. ULTIMATELY, THOUGH, IT WAS THE CRUSADE THAT BECAME THE STUFF OF LEGEND, THE CRUSADE OF KING RICHARD THE LIONHEART OF ENGLAND AGAINST THE FORMIDABLE SALADIN.

Introduction

As the news of the fall of Jerusalem spread across the European continent it was greeted with both dismay and surprise. Regular news of the turbulent conditions in the East had not led people to expect that things were really as bad as they had turned out to be. The instant response the Latin Christians might have hoped for was unlikely, since Crusades, after the Second Crusade, were now regarded, in effect, as the sport of kings. As such, the leading participants of the Third Crusade would need to put their own affairs in order before coming to the aid of the East.

It was fortunate that King William II of Sicily immediately sent a fleet to help the beleaguered Christian coastal fortresses. Even more fortunate had been the chance arrival of Conrad of Montferrat at Tyre within two weeks of the Battle of Hattin. Unaware of the calamities that had befallen the Franks, Conrad would be instrumental in the defence of that city against the forces of Saladin.

The first army of the Third Crusade to arrive in the East was that of the holy Roman emperor, Frederick Barbarossa. It was a huge

edeuch qup deptue fut empeur :
et eftort frere du 3i roy lossome
non obstant sa ionesse retouuera tout se

◄ The holy Roman emperor, Frederick Barbarossa, departs for the Third Crusade in 1189.

force of men. The traditional chaos had broken out on their way to Constantinople, much to the chagrin of those princes unfortunate

▲ Frederick had a stroke while bathing in a stream in Asia Minor.

enough to have lands in the path of the army. Things were no different in Constantinople, where Emperor Isaac Angelus' treaty with Saladin, brokered primarily to keep the Seljuks at bay while he dealt with the Norman foe in Greece, was as popular with the Germans as Frederick's suggestion for a Crusade against Constantinople had been with the Byzantines.

What this huge German force under its old and wily emperor might have achieved will never be known, since Frederick was destined never to encounter Saladin's forces. He died on the journey to the Holy Land and, deprived of his leadership, the army fell apart under the traditional assaults of the East—Muslim skirmishers and disease. The bedraggled force that arrived in the Holy Land bore no comparison to the army that had set out months earlier. It was still accompanied by Frederick, pickled in vinegar by his companions, who were determined that he should fulfill his vow to enter the Holy City. Thus he arrived at Antioch in a barrel, although the heat and buffeting of the journey had managed to undo the preservative powers of the vinegar. What remained was discreetly buried there, but a few of his followers, loyal to the last, removed a few bones to take with them on the journey south.

A crusade is launched

King Philip II of France, whose military technology assisted Conrad in the siege of Tyre.

In the Holy Land the Germans were to meet up with new forces sent from Europe under the command of two kings: Richard I of England, the Lionheart, and Philip II of France. Of the two, Richard was the military man—he had recently attained the crown of England but had spent many of his years as a prince in combat, sometimes fighting against his own father's forces. Although younger than Richard, Philip had ruled France for a decade and was the model of a medieval king.

By this time, Saladin had released King Guy. The Muslim leader, mistaking kingship for honor, had extracted a promise from Guy that he would take no further part in the conflict. Guy had reneged on this promise at the earliest opportunity. When he reached Tyre, however, a surprise was in store for him. Conrad considered the city he had saved to be his own and, no doubt mindful of Guy's reputation, prevented him from entering. Guy and the forces he then managed to attract set off to attack Acre, keen to obtain a base from which the retrieval of his lost kingdom could be planned. Conrad joined him there later and a peace was agreed between the two kings as they united to retake the city.

Conrad had brought Philip of France with him. In April 1191 they landed at Acre to join the siege. Apart from the extra men and ships he brought, Philip had experts in siege technology with him, men whose knowledge of the trebuchet, the mangonel, and other such catapults was to prove invaluable. One catapult, God's Own Sling, was already engaged in pounding the Muslim walls; the addition of the Evil Neighbor would further interrupt their already troubled sleep.

RICHARD 1.er
(RICHARD CŒUR DE LION)

◀ King Richard I of England, the Lionheart, one of the most renowned of all leaders of the Crusades.

Richard, meanwhile, had been detained. Bad weather had forced some of his ships to seek a safe haven at Cyprus, which had recovered somewhat from Reynald's earlier attack. A Byzantine, Isaac Ducas Comnenus, had rebelled against his emperor, claiming the title for himself, and now ruled the island independently. The hollowness of his claim was illustrated by the ease with which Richard dealt with him. One of the ships that had landed had both Richard's sister and his fiancée—Berengaria of Navarre—on board. Isaac obviously thought that the women, with their obvious potential as hostages, provided rich fruit for the picking. Isaac, unaware of Richard's nature, made the worst decision possible. While failing to capture either of the women he displayed enough bad faith to antagonize Richard when he appeared with the rest of the fleet. That King Guy and his leading barons had arrived pleading for Richard's help with the siege now taking place at Acre was of no importance. Richard flatly stated that Cyprus was of inestimable value to the Crusader cause. Isaac, for all his bravado, was swiftly overcome and taken prisoner. The natives rejoiced at the fall of a disliked leader. Richard left two of his men in charge and then set off for Acre, accompanied by Guy, his men, and the imprisoned former "emperor." Local joy soon disappeared when the inhabitants were taxed to new levels and, more unforgivably in their eyes, legally shorn of the symbol of Eastern manhood—their beards.

Upon Richard's arrival the rulers of Acre despaired. The men and arms

◀ Richard the Lionheart of England lands at Jaffa at the head of a large army of Crusaders.

▼ The city of Acre is taken by the Crusaders on July 12th, 1191.

▶ God's Own Sling, a huge catapult, was a tactical weapon contributed to the Crusade by Philip II of France.

now set against them were considerable. The Franks and their allies were at first held up by disease—Philip and Richard both fell prey—and then by the inevitable bickering as Guy won Richard over to his cause and Conrad recruited Philip to his. However, this did not hold them up for long. In July, Acre surrendered, offering up a fortune for the safety of its inhabitants. Saladin cursed his bad luck, unable to come to its rescue in time.

Once Acre was captured, the arguments between Guy and Conrad resumed. Guy, never popular, had found his hold on the throne loosened by the death of his wife, who had provided his claim. Conrad, cunningly, had married her sister in the meantime, and thus the Latin barons who favored him, or, rather, who detested Guy, had a legitimate argument for calling for his leadership. Finally it was decided that Conrad would remain ruler of Beirut, Sidon, and Tyre and that he, or his family, should he predecease them, would inherit the kingship on Guy's death.

The internal conflict between these rulers, despite their perilous standing, could not have impressed their potential saviors from the West. Philip had soon had enough of the East. He decided, despite the arguments to the contrary, to set out for home, leaving Richard in charge. Richard had had enough too—of Acre. Unable to reach an accommodation with Saladin and keen to push on to Jerusalem, he had the thousands of prisoners taken during the siege killed. The Muslims were outraged. As the Crusaders slowly moved down

▼ Acre surrenders to Richard the Lionheart and Philip of France.

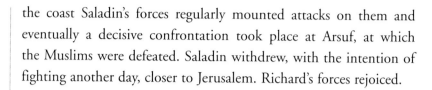
The city of Acre today.

Crusader and Muslim forces in the thick of battle at Arsuf, September 7th, 1191.

the coast Saladin's forces regularly mounted attacks on them and eventually a decisive confrontation took place at Arsuf, at which the Muslims were defeated. Saladin withdrew, with the intention of fighting another day, closer to Jerusalem. Richard's forces rejoiced.

Months later, in 1192, Jerusalem had still not been taken. The joy engendered by the previous year's victory had been replaced by sober thought. Richard was confident that he could take the Holy City. What was in doubt was whether, once taken, it could be held. Saladin's forces had been proven not to be invincible. What was beyond question was that the native Christian forces could not hold on to much more than the coastal fortresses without a permanent and sizeable contribution from the West. Richard, however, had no intention of staying. He was there for the glory, for the riches to be won in battle—not for the burden of administering and maintaining a Latin Kingdom. Negotiations with the Muslim enemy were protracted; news began to arrive of troubles back home in England; Cyprus was proving to be a hot potato. Richard sold the island to the Templars, hoping to rid himself of its troubles. Then the Templars tried to sell it back to him. Richard took it upon himself to make Conrad king in the Holy Land and to arrange Guy's accession to the throne of Cyprus. Conrad's joy was short-lived. He was struck down by agents of the Assassins not far from the safety of his palace one

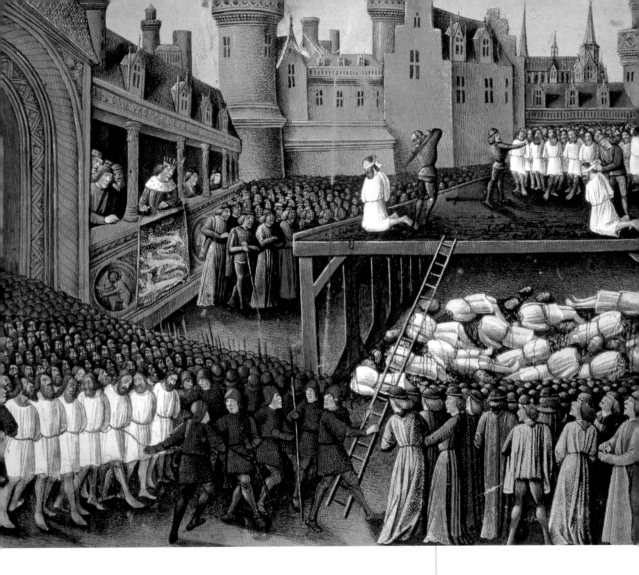

April evening. The hand behind the blade was the subject of much speculation that year, with conspiracy theories abounding. Conrad's widow, Isabella, married a newcomer, Henry of Champagne, within days of her husband's death. It was Henry who would benefit from Richard's interference in the Latin succession.

Still, Richard delayed his departure. His next move was to conquer the Muslim coastal fortress of Daron. The Christians now held a kingdom that stretched along the lengthy coast, a territory that was no wider than a ribbon. For all his meager talents as a king, Richard

▲ After Acre was taken by the Crusaders, Richard dealt brutally with the survivors, executing thousands of Muslim prisoners.

▲ Richard had a worthy opponent in Saladin, and fought fiercely against him in every confrontation.

had proved one thing. As had been the case with the Muslims, a single, undisputed leader brought tremendous benefit to the Frankish cause. The rival barons might still plot against one another but Richard's presence had curtailed the extremes of their behavior. The unfortunate realization that came with this was that it was now difficult to see how Europe could hold on to the Holy Land beyond the short term. The lessons of recent history must have made it clear to Saladin that he did not need so much to engage in a war of aggression as to play a waiting game. Richard weakened his own situation when he allowed news of his intention to leave to spread. Knowing this, Saladin was able to play for time. Even without this knowledge, it must have been apparent that any major force sent from Europe would, by its very nature, be merely a temporary upset. The reality was that under a single leader, the Muslims would inevitably reclaim the Frankish kingdoms. A war fought overseas for ideological reasons would always be difficult to win. The Muslims had nowhere else to go. The Franks would never be in the ascendant without outside help from their fellow Christians, whose hearts and homes would always remain in Europe.

Despite Richard's declared intention to leave, and the endless negotiations, his finest hour as a military leader was yet to come. In 1192, hearing of an attack on Jaffa by Saladin's armies, Richard rushed to the scene with a smaller force. He not only recaptured the city but also, in the following days, withstood an attack by Saladin's numerically superior army, who were trying to crush him before the arrival of his reinforcements. Richard's behavior here was indeed heroic—he appeared wherever he was needed, without any thought of the risk to himself. His older opponent could not but admire the man's courage, however much he despised his cruelty. However, this event was to be the final act of the Third Crusade. In the negotiations that followed the demands made by Saladin could not be refused by a king so anxious about the state of his own country in his absence. A peace was agreed, allowing for both Christians and Muslims to move freely. Although Richard had been unable to take Jerusalem, he now ensured that Christians would be able to worship there, and pilgrims would be permitted to visit the city. Having achieved that much, Richard finally departed for England. His journey home took a considerable length of time—he was captured first by the Austrians and then the Germans. When he arrived back in 1194, it was to the news that Saladin had finally succumbed to a fatal illness more than a year earlier.

After Saladin's death, the Muslim sense of unity disappeared. His lands were divided among his many sons and their internecine plotting gave valuable breathing space to the Latin Kingdoms. Saladin's brother, al-Adil, struggled to keep his young nephews in line. Henry of Champagne, despite marrying Isabella, was never crowned king. In the years that followed he did his best to maintain the Frankish territory. The Assassins once more came on board. In the north the Armenians worried at Antioch with the tacit approval of the Christians in the south. Henry's one major antagonist within his own borders, Amalric of Lusignan, in control of Acre, relinquished that territory when his elder brother, Guy of Cyprus, died in 1194, leaving the throne of the island vacant. Amalric withdrew there, biding his time. His opportunity did not take long to arrive. In 1197, Henry died when he accidentally stepped back through the open window of an upper level of his palace in Acre. The only help to hand was his loyal dwarf who, grasping hold of his beloved leader, took that loyalty to the grave—both men plummeted to their deaths, several stories below. Amalric stepped forward to take the once-again widowed Isabella's hand, to general approbation.

That same year a force of Germans arrived, eager to rescue their reputation from the debacle of their role in the Third Crusade. They showed the traditional respect for the wisdom of the Christian rulers they found there and sought out the Infidel as early as they could. By the close of the following year, most of them had returned to Europe. They had contributed to the taking of Beirut, a victory that owed more to the incompetence of those holding that city than to any military genius on the part of the Franks. Apart from that single success, they had achieved nothing and the German contribution to the Frankish cause remained as ridiculed as it had been when they arrived. Some were sufficiently shamed to stay and, working with a hospice set up by German merchants in Acre, formed yet another military order—the Teutonic Knights, with the intention

▼ Beirut falls to the Crusaders in 1197, the single success in the campaign fought by the German crusading force.

of providing help and actually adding further dissent in an already factionalized series of campaigns. As the new century dawned, news of another European crusade began to reach the East.

If the Third Crusade could be pointed to as the event where myths of the valiant Crusader had at least some basis in fact, the Fourth could be described as the campaign where the Crusaders lost focus. In 1202 the Fourth Crusade was officially launched as an attempt to recover Jerusalem. It soon descended into an opportunity to deal with the heretics in Constantinople.

The next decade was remarkable for a series of crusades against everybody but the Muslims: the cross was taken up not only against the Byzantines but also in the Baltic, and, in 1209, against Cathar heretics in France. The one attempt against the Muslims was, bizarrely, made by children.

▲ Hermann von Salza, the fourth grand master of the Order of the Teutonic Knights, is given the papal seal by Pope Innocent III.

7 The Fourth Crusade and the Children's Crusade

THE NOBLES WHO RESPONDED TO THE CALL FOR A FOURTH CRUSADE WERE INSPIRED LESS BY THE NEED TO DEFEAT THE INFIDEL THAN BY THE DESIRE TO BRING EASTERN HERETICS INTO LINE, FILLING THEIR OWN POCKETS AT THE SAME TIME. HOWEVER, A CHILDREN'S CRUSADE SET OUT IN 1212 WITH THE SAME AIMS AS THOSE OF THE ORIGINAL CRUSADES.

Introduction

A new pope, Innocent III, strongly supported the idea of a new crusade. Preachers, fired up with the customary crusading zeal, went up and down France and Germany, preaching the cross. The concerns of kings were largely elsewhere but many barons flocked to the cause, hungry for land and booty elsewhere. The absence of any major figure to lead the effort would soon become noticeable. One group wanted to attack Egypt, seeing it as the key to a successful reconquest; another, for political reasons, wanted to attack Constantinople to replace the current ruler there. The Byzantine Empire's continued decline had made it impossible to follow the traditional overland route to the East. The only feasible way was by sea. The Italian republics were the only possible carriers and the Venetians offered the solution. Venice was enjoying great success. With no concern

▼ Pope Innocent III preaches the Fourth Crusade at the Lateran Council in Rome in 1215.

out money, they were prepared to make any kind of deal with any kind of person. In Constantinople they bought trading rights cheaply, playing on the desperate need for money there. In the Levant, they carried essentials to the Franks and relieved them of their Eastern luxuries. In Egypt they negotiated with the Muslims, keen to raise funds themselves. Venice had a finger in every pie. When the crusading transport deal was done, however, the Venetians suddenly found themselves struggling to find a place to deliver the fighters where their own interests would not be likely to suffer. After much procrastination, they tried to convince the Crusaders to start their campaign by reclaiming Venetian territory that had fallen to the Hungarians—who were fellow Christians—along the Dalmatian coast and, in particular, the city of Zara. Faced with bankruptcy if they had to pay for a prolonged stay in Venice, or with the prospect of finding an alternative route to Jerusalem that didn't involve Venetian ships, the Crusaders had no choice but to acquiesce. They sacked Zara in 1202. When news came back to Innocent that his holy army's first act had been against Christians he showed his great displeasure by excommunicating those he held responsible. Both the Venetians and the Crusaders were punished in this way. The Crusaders' excommunication, however, was soon rescinded when Innocent calmed down and realized both that they had been given no other option by their hosts and that the army could hardly continue its campaign in the absence of papal support. Innocent's control of the campaign, however, had been shown to be illusory.

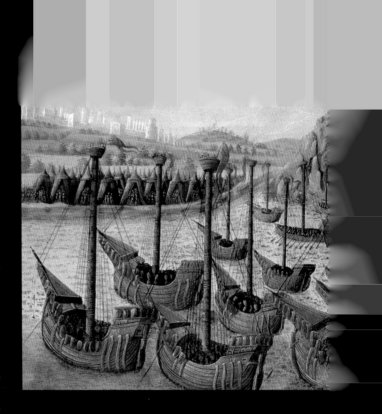

▲ A fleet of Crusaders arrives at Constantinople in 1203 to win the city for Alexius IV, son of the deposed emperor, Isaac.

The Fourth Crusade

Behind the push toward Constantinople was Philip of Swabia, whose wife was the daughter-in-law of the displaced emperor of the Byzantines. Restoring her family to the throne there might cement Philip's position and give him the opportunity to make a little bit of money at the same time. He had already been excommunicated prior to the conquest of Zara, so what more could the pope do? The crusading army, despite everything it had done for them in Zara, still owed a debt to its host and transporters. The Venetians began to see the appeal of a redirection toward Constantinople. Why should they pay for the right to trade when they could persuade the Crusaders to fight for that right for them, and, in addition, convince them to pay the Venetians for the opportunity to do it? For now the Venetians pressed their claims strongly, and news that the pretender to the Byzantine throne would pay their debts swayed many otherwise upright Crusaders. The few that had rectitude enough—or at least the money to afford such a thing—paid their own way to Syria. The rest set off, under Venetian sails, toward Constantinople. Innocent was rendered powerless to alter the course of his instrument of salvation.

After a few attempts by the Crusaders, the incumbent emperor, Alexius III, fled. Philip's cousin by marriage was raised to the throne as Alexius IV, sharing it with his father, the tortured and blinded former emperor, Isaac, who had been released from the Byzantine jails by those left in charge of the city after the departure of Alexius III. Alexius IV's joy was brought to an end when he tried to pay the Crusaders and, through them, the Venetians, and discovered that the money wasn't there. He tried to introduce harsh taxes to placate the confident Westerners who now walked through the city as if it were their own. His people rioted. A new emperor, Alexius V, was installed and Alexius IV and Isaac were imprisoned and tortured to death. If this had meant that their money would have been forthcoming the Crusaders would probably not have objected. As it was, they decided that the only emperor of Constantinople who could be trusted to pay up would be a Western one.

In the end, it took the Crusaders relatively little effort to break the city. Once in, they unleashed their pent-up aggression in a way that was to make the Byzantines wish that they had been conquered by Muslims rather than by Christians. Alexius V had fled by the time the barbarians poured in. For three days they ravaged the city. They raped the women, and killed the men and the children; they stole everything they could, and they destroyed everything else. Much is made of what was lost in the final sack of Constantinople by the Ottoman Sultan Mehmed II in 1453, but the damage done in 1204 was greater. The ancient statue of Athena by Phidias, a sculpture that dated back to the Athens of Socrates and Plato, was broken up by supporters of Alexius V in his efforts to supplant the previous ruler. Its destruction was an omen of the devastation to come. The Venetians and the barons leading the Crusade finally reined in their troops when they realized that they would have nothing left if the rampage continued. They elected a ruler, Baldwin of Flanders, pragmatically supported by the Venetians as a

▼ Alexis IV makes the case for the assistance of the Crusaders in freeing his father, the deposed Emperor Isaac.

▶ Constantinople is captured by the
Crusaders on April 13th, 1204.

candidate too weak to oppose their activities in the lands that he was to rule. For the next few years many more of the great treasures of Constantinople flooded onto the European market.

The Venetians claimed parts of Constantinople, the western coast of Greece, and many of its islands. Baldwin, in addition, sold them Crete. The Venetians were content to franchise out almost all of the islands of the Aegean. Mainland Greece was entirely given over to Westerners. There was now a duke of Athens from Burgundy and a prince of Achaea from France. In the northwest, in Epirus, one Byzantine lord held out. In the east a host of small Byzantine states claimed independence—Nicaea and Trebizond, on the Black Sea, among others. With these bastions of Byzantine power intact, the population of Constantinople could always hold out hope that one day a Byzantine would again occupy the throne.

▶ Baldwin of Flanders is crowned Baldwin I, Emperor of Byzantium, by Venetian Doge Enrico Dandolo.

When Innocent heard about this it put him in a difficult position. His anger at the direction the Crusade had taken was subdued by his joy at the final reduction of the Byzantine heresy. Rome stood unchallenged. However, when news of the sack of the city and the barbarous behavior displayed by the Crusaders arrived he was shocked. News of how cunningly the Venetians had exploited the situation fueled his anger. Still, he had the hope that now the real job could continue. When he found out that his own legate on the Crusade had announced that the successful capture of the Byzantine Empire meant that those who had made the promise to go to the Latin Kingdoms to rescue Jerusalem could now go home, it must have been the final straw for the pope. The Fourth Crusade was officially over.

In the East, the non-appearance of the rumored Great Crusade was now explained by the news that had begun to come through to both the Muslims and Christians there. Peace reigned for the present. Amalric had come to an agreement with al-Adil. Each had his preoccupations. Amalric died in 1205 with the peace still in force. News of the taking of Constantinople not only meant the end to any immediate help for the Franks, it also provided a magnet for those minor nobility in the Latin Kingdoms who had still failed to make their name and fortune. Land and opportunity beckoned much closer to Europe, in the western parts of the old empire, now renamed Romania by its conquerors. How much easier a prospect that must have seemed than continuing to hope against hope for something to turn up in the Muslim badlands. Knights began to make their way to the "new" empire. The wisest among the Franks received the news of the independent Byzantine states with dismay. After the sack of their capital, how could these rulers wish for anything else but the destruction of Western hopes in the Latin Kingdoms of the East? In addition, how could any future crusade ever make its way across Asia Minor? It was not quite the end—but where could they go from here?

The Children's Crusade

The Crusades were not necessarily an endeavor limited to the nobility. An inspirational speaker from any class could do his bit to contribute to the cause. Peter the Hermit, the inspiration behind the First Crusade, provided an example for other evangelists of the lower orders after his death, and itinerant preachers who delivered this message were now a common fact of life, particularly among the towns and villages of Europe. Into this fervid arena came a 12-year-old boy, Stephen, a French shepherd by trade, who claimed to have encountered Christ and to have been given a letter from him that authorized his role as a preacher of the Crusade that was destined to win back the Holy Land. The French king, Philip, had little time for such nonsense and sent the child packing. Swiftly and inexplicably news of his mission spread and soon children across France were laying down their hoes and flocking to the banner of one who was prophesying an army of children before whom the Mediterranean would part and the Saracen would lay down his arms. Germany was not to be outdone—a child by the name of Nicholas began to preach there. Tens of thousands of children were soon migrating south.

▼ Thousands of French and German children, singing hymns, set out on their own crusade in 1212.

The French arrived at Marseilles; the Germans, in different waves, passed through Switzerland and eventually ended up at Genoa and Pisa. The Mediterranean unhelpfully refused to divide at either port. The German armies of children, and the dubious characters who followed in their wake, soon broke up in the face of the sea's obduracy. Many had died or had been lost on the journey, although a few of the wealthiest managed to obtain passage to the Holy Land at Genoa and Pisa. More went on to Rome, obtaining an audience with the pope, who indulged their fervor, promising that, when older, their commitment to the crusading cause would be allowed to blossom. Satisfied, they broke up to seek their immediate fortune elsewhere. Some embarked on the dangerous journey home; others chose to stay in Italy, seeking something better than the grim lives from which they had escaped in Germany. The few parents who did get their children back were outnumbered by the angry many who, unable to seek redress in any other manner, chose to salve their wounds by hanging Nicholas' father for allowing his son to start such an escapade.

▲ A young French shepherd, Stephen, enlists boys and girls to the youthful crusading army.

Unfortunately for the French, a couple of enterprising merchants in Marseilles offered to provide the children's passage to Palestine. William the Pig and Hugh the Iron lived up to their word, selling off the children to the Muslims as slaves. Twenty years passed before rumors of the young pilgrims' fate in Egypt, Baghdad, and throughout the Maghrib made their way back to those few of their parents who were still alive.

8 The Fifth, Sixth, and Seventh Crusades

THE FIRST HALF OF THE THIRTEENTH CENTURY SAW THE LAUNCH OF NO FEWER THAN THREE CRUSADES. ONLY THE SECOND OF THESE, THE SEVENTH CRUSADE, LED BY THE HOLY ROMAN EMPEROR FREDERICK II, COULD BE VIEWED AS HAVING ACHIEVED A MEASURE OF SUCCESS.

Introduction

The savior of the Fifth Crusade was always hoped to be Frederick II, the German holy Roman emperor. Instead, his was to be the deciding role in the Sixth Crusade. Inspired by Richard of England's earlier observation that Egypt was the key to the retrieval of the Latin territories, the Fifth Crusade started in northern Egypt—and it ended there. At the heart of the Fifth Crusade is yet another tale of split leadership. The Muslims were too divided to repel the invaders easily. After their initial gains, the Christians were too disunited to get any farther. A strong papal representative, Pelagius, presumed himself to be in charge and provided a constant impediment to the overall military leader, John of Brienne. John was a latecomer to the East. Upon Amalric's death in 1174, the crown

▼ Emperor Frederick II receives a delegation of Muslims at his court in Palermo in 1230.

of Jerusalem had briefly passed back to his widow, Isabella; on her death her eldest daughter, Maria, still in her teens, took the throne, and John of Brienne, Lord of Beirut, was appointed regent. John of Brienne was already an old man when he was pushed forward by Philip of France as a suitable husband for the teenage queen. He quickly adapted to the political realities of the East; his age, perhaps, encouraged a certain circumspection on his part. His modest achievements were shown in a favorable light when compared to the situation to the north.

▲ The city of Antioch, impregnable until the siege in 1098, continued to have a strategic role.

Antioch was in a mess. The legitimacy of its ruler, Bohemond IV, was challenged by the claims of his nephew, Raymond. Raymond would have provided a minor obstacle, but his case was backed by his relative, the powerful Armenian lord, Leo. Every force involved in the area soon found itself on one side or the other. The Templars, the Seljuk Turks, and the Antiochene Greeks supported Bohemond; the Hospitalers and al-Adil were behind Leo. Leo cleverly put the Armenian Church under the pope. Bohemond sided with the Greek Church. The pope excommunicated Bohemond and Antioch, then the Churches switched their allegiances. The Templars' role as Christian supremacists was now challenged by extremist behavior from the Hospitalers, who had begun to use the Assassins as tools. They murdered Bohemond's eldest son in church and then killed the patriarch of Jerusalem. A measure of calm was restored only when Raymond took control in a coup in Antioch while Bohemond was struggling to put down a revolt in his other territory, Tripoli. The whole episode was a perfect example of interests taking

The Fifth Crusade

That John of Brienne, a lowly member of the French nobility, was to take command of the Crusade is a comment on the tenacity of kings. Frederick II never joined the Fifth Crusade. The young king of Cyprus, Hugh, died on the way there. King Andrew of Hungary treated the whole thing as a vacation—the petrified head of St. Stephen was his main souvenir, brought back to Hungary before the attack on Egypt had even been launched. The forces that landed in Egypt in 1218 were a combination of French, Austrians, members of the military orders (Templars, Hospitalers, and Teutonic Knights),

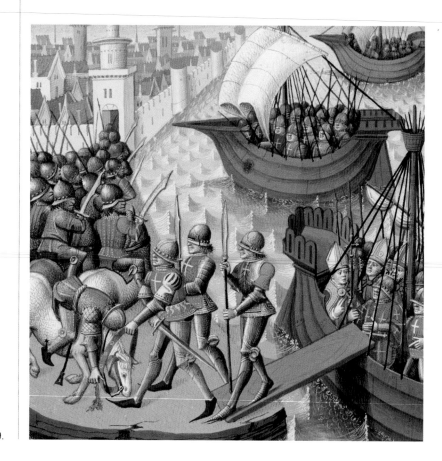

▶ Crusaders arrive at Damietta by boat, the best way to reach the fortress, which was almost completely seabound.

▶▶ The city of Damietta is finally captured by the Crusaders in 1219.

natives of Outremer, and a smattering of others. Their plan was to take the fortress of Damietta close to the coast where its branch of the Nile flowed into the sea. It was on a piece of land almost entirely surrounded by water, with the river to the west and the great Lake Manzaleh to the east. Damietta didn't fall until November 1219, when the Crusaders finally broke in to find a community wasted by disease and death. Beyond this, little was achieved. A final push south was made in 1221, when the Christians took Sharimshah.

John argued that they should stop and consolidate; Pelagius demanded that they push on. When they did they found themselves surrounded. The Nile had risen as it did seasonally each year; the Muslims opened the gates holding the water back. The Crusaders fell back in confusion, flooded and harried by the Muslim forces. Pelagius was forced to sue for peace and the Fifth Crusade ended when the Christians left in their ships in September, 1221.

Opportunities had frequently been presented to the Crusaders. More than once the Muslims had offered to cede Jerusalem and its environs to the Christians during the campaign. Pelagius had always refused. John's attempts to take command were in part hindered by his worries back home in Outremer. In addition the legitimacy of his leadership was regularly undermined by Pelagius, with his constant taunts that soon a real ruler, Frederick II, would come to take command. A greater man than John might have firmly sidelined Pelagius and, having done so, would have had a real chance to take control of Egypt. The thought must have occurred to the Crusaders who survived as they set sail for Europe. One great man had been present among the Christians—Francis of Assisi had arrived in an attempt to bring peace in 1219. The Muslim leader, the Sultan al-Kamil, listened to his entreaties, offered him gifts, and then sent him on his way. It was probably a more gracious reception than the one he received from his own side.

◀ St. Francis of Assissi tries to persuade Sultan Melik al-Kamil to embrace the teachings of Christianity.

The Sixth Crusade

Frederick II made a promise to take up the cross at his coronation as holy Roman emperor.

The days of the early Crusades now seemed to have been simpler times. There had always been internal conflicts on both sides but, in general, there had been a more straightforward set of circumstances in place. Each subsequent attempt muddied the waters of the East. The alliance between Assassins and Hospitalers would have been unthinkable generations earlier. It is, perhaps, noteworthy that the final recapture of Jerusalem would fall to a man who, more than any other, encapsulated the complexities of the time. The brief resurgence in Christian fortunes would be brought about by a figure best described in modern terms as an antihero.

Frederick II was an extraordinary figure: he truly contained multitudes. He was raised in Sicily and elected king there at the age of three. Sicily's multicultural heritage informed his development. His brilliant mind soaked up whatever he was exposed to—he became fluent in Arabic, French, German, Greek, Italian, and Latin. His exposure to the Islamic heritage of that island and his genius provided him with the mindset to deal with the Muslims of the East in a manner more common among the native Christian leaders of Outremer. In this he was unique as a Western leader. Typical of the contradictions within him were that, as the greatest secular defender of the faith, he employed a bodyguard of Saracens—who were, by definition, immune to papal seduction—before he ever set foot in Outremer. His greatest flaws were mixed in with his strengths in the way in which he transcended the typical European king. Frederick saw himself as above everyone, including the pope. If he had been born emperor of the Byzantines it would have been a different matter. If the papacy had been weaker and if the lesser kings and nobility had not grown used to the powers and privileges they enjoyed in the thirteenth century, then his achievements might have been more lasting.

◄ Frederick II is crowned in the cathedral at Palermo, Sicily, in 1197. His mother Constance, seen here holding the boy, was instrumental in his accession to the throne of Sicily.

That his success in the East was limited is perhaps understandable when it is considered that he viewed the papacy, rather than Islam, as the real villain. And the papacy's later description of him as antichrist is testimony to the extent to which it regarded him as a threat to the Church.

The first half of Frederick's life story is the account of his struggle to regain his father's position as holy Roman emperor. His coronation as emperor involved a promise to take up the cross. While his old tutor, Honorius III, was pope, Frederick's protestations of needing to put his own lands in order before sorting out others fell on friendly ears. When Honorius died, and the new pope, Gregory IX, was elected,

▶ Frederick is crowned emperor by Pope Honorius III on November 22nd, 1220.

it became clear that this argument would no longer be effective. Gregory insisted that he go. When malaria afflicted both Frederick and the army he had gathered, Gregory promptly excommunicated him for his dilatoriness. It is ironic that at this point the Sultan al-Kamil, one of the architects of the repulsion of the Fifth Crusade, was in secret communication with Frederick. He, too, urged the emperor to come to the Holy Land, hoping that Frederick would join forces with him against a threat to his own security from the east.

Frederick did not allow his excommunication to stand in his way, despite the fact that, technically, it made him ineligible to take part in a Crusade. Since his election as emperor, he now also had a per-

▶ Frederick, seen here with his young wife at his side, had a well-deserved reputation for bullying his barons.

sonal interest in Outremer. In 1222, John of Brienne had journeyed to Europe to seek support for Outremer and, in particular, to ensure the succession by finding a husband for his daughter, Yolanda, now queen after the death of her mother. Frederick seemed the perfect choice—a decision that was encouraged by the pope as one likely to hurry the emperor's journey to the east. Once the marriage had taken place, Frederick sent his young bride to Sicily, where she remained for the rest of her short life. John found that he was surplus to requirements and, when the opportunity arose for him to act as regent at Constantinople, he quickly accepted. He could thus claim the throne of Jerusalem by right before leaving Europe.

When Frederick arrived in the Levant in 1228, his claim had effectively vanished. Yolanda's death after giving birth to their son, Conrad, was now common knowledge, and the throne was rightfully in the possession of the infant—Frederick was merely regent until Conrad came of age. To Frederick this was of little importance, since he was the *de facto* ruler. To the barons of Outremer, it was of the greatest importance. Before even reaching Acre, Frederick was flexing his muscle. When he arrived at Cyprus he demanded to see the leading nobles of both the island and the mainland. He was, after all, holy Roman emperor and thus overlord of the island. His bullying manner with the barons had had an unsettling effect on them and would prove to be counterproductive. Later they would look for any excuse not to cooperate with him, while being wary of deliberate and obvious disobedience. The perfect excuse came soon after he arrived at Acre. News began to drift in that, not content with his first excommunication of the emperor for his failure to leave for the East promptly enough, Gregory had excommunicated him a second time for daring to go on a Crusade while excommunicated. Regardless of Gregory's logic, or of queries about how an excommunicant could be excommunicated, this provided the barons with a means of legally shunning him. Certainly the Templars and Hospitalers were keen not to earn the pope's enmity—though the Teutonic Knights, with their German origins, were placed in a very difficult situation of divided loyalties.

Frederick, however, had his friends to fall back on—not surprisingly, they were all German, and too few to provide an army of sufficient size to retake Jerusalem by force. Frederick must have wondered what he had become entangled in. To be ruler of the Holy Land, to be the one who took back Jerusalem was fodder for his ego and a powerful

▼ Pope Gregory IX insisted that Frederick live up to his coronation promise to take up the cross, and excommunicated the emperor when he failed to embark on a Crusade.

◀ The city of Jerusalem, its skyline dominated by the mosque of the Dome of the Rock.

boost to his prestige in his battle against the one figure he felt was a threat to his role as the lord of Christian Europe—the pope. Now that he was actually in Outremer, the material benefits must have seemed slight. He had effectively outmaneuvered himself by his own actions. He could not move forward, nor could he retreat without a huge loss of face. The only recourse that was open to him was negotiation with the enemy.

▼ The interior of the Dome of the Rock mosque.

Fortunately for Frederick, Sultan al-Kamil shared his pragmatism. Al-Kamil was preoccupied with the familiar concern of unification—in his case, of the separate Ayubite territories. In addition, he was still concerned about the threat from the east, from Jelal ad-Din and his Khwarismian Turks, who had recently defeated the new threat coming out of the Far East, the Mongols. Al-Kamil and Frederick held each other in mutual respect. Handing over Jerusalem and a few of the other sites, Bethlehem and Nazareth among them, was a negligible cost if it allowed al-Kamil to forget about any Frankish threat. However, ensuring the Muslim possession of the Islamic sites within Jerusalem, such as the Dome of the Rock and the area around the Temple, was essential to his reputation. What did this matter to Frederick? Al-Kamil also played safe by offering only the tiniest strip of land to link these places with the Latin coast. It would be an impossible territory to defend, should he ever desire to retake

these places. This was of no consequence to Frederick, since it gave him the solution to his immediate problems, particularly if it took care of his critics. On February 18th, 1229, the agreement was signed, and for the last time, Jerusalem passed back into the ownership of the West. Al-Kamil and Frederick celebrated the fruition of their plan.

Unity between Muslim and Christian at this level had never occurred in the East until this point. Now a common response issued from both sides. Pious believers across the divide were incensed. Al-Kamil faced harsh criticism from his own people over the cowardly seceding of Islamic territory to unbelievers. Frederick faced even more abuse. That he had won such an indefensible territory, saddling them with

a strategic nightmare, greatly angered the native barons; that he had left the Muslims in control of parts of Jerusalem seemed an act of treachery to the truest of believers; that he had outwitted the Church and, despite two excommunications, had actually won back the jewel of the Christian East enraged the Roman Church. The patriarch of Jerusalem, Gerold of Lausanne, was moved to immediate action. A third excommunication was unlikely to have any effect on Frederick, so Gerold declared that if Jerusalem were to receive its regent and liberator, he would place an interdict upon the whole city, banning any church ceremony or acts taking place there until further notice.

Frederick went to the city, and, in spite of his son's claim, declared himself king of Jerusalem. He had to crown himself as no priest would perform the ceremony. After the ceremony, Frederick went on a walk around his kingdom. When he noticed a priest following him into a Muslim holy place he ordered the man removed and declared that anyone who entered in future without Muslim approval would be executed. In the Dome of the Rock there was a grille that was explained as being necessary to keep the sparrows out of the building. Using a Muslim description for Christians he remarked that, "God has now sent you pigs." News of this, and of his self-enthronement, added to the odium in which he was held by the Franks.

Frederick retired, exasperated by the ungrateful response. News of problems in his European lands began to reach him. The pope was taking advantage of his absence to make a move on his Italian possessions. Frederick, after making public his plans to leave, tried to slip away unnoticed under the cover of darkness. News of his departure spread and, such was the hatred felt toward him, even by commoners, that he was forced to flee for his ship under an unholy rain of excrement and rotting offal hurled by the crowd.

◀ In the absence of a compliant priest, Frederick crowns himself king of Jerusalem.

So ended the Sixth Crusade.

The Seventh Crusade

After Frederick left, although the barons attempted to rebuild the defences around Jerusalem and the other sites he had regained, many of their fears were realized. It was impossible to defend much of the territory from the depredations of bandits and bands of Muslims angered by al-Kamil's perfidy. Back in Europe, Frederick had managed to come to a temporary understanding with the pope in 1230. Divisions existed between the commanders he had left and the native barons, led by the powerful and respected John of Ibelin, ruler of Beirut, who was in league with the young King Henry of Cyprus. Attempts were made to dispute Frederick's kingship in Jerusalem, particularly by Queen Alice of Cyprus. With the death of John in a riding accident, and the absence of the true king, Conrad, Frederick's infant son, practical government was in the hands of the commune of Acre—a group of leading barons and merchants in the chief Latin city. This control was disputed by Frederick's appointed representatives, or *bailli*, who endeavored to rule in his name. Particularly hated was Richard Filangieri, sent by Frederick from Italy in 1231—he achieved the feat of bringing the Templars and Hospitalers together in common cause against him. To the north, too, in Antioch, a commune made most of the decisions, regardless of the desires expressed by their weak lord, Bohemond V.

▼ Members of the Order of the Temple, founded in 1119. This military order included not only the famed knights of the Crusades, but monks and friars as well.

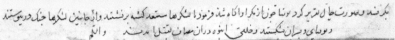

بكرنده وصورت جال لغديد كرد دونا خون از بكر اداكاه شد فرمودا شكرها ستعد كشة ر شنتد وازجانب شكرها جنك درتوشتند
دومهاي ودران بكشتد وخلتي ابوه دران معان فتلا يدسته والله

◄ Mongol warriors on horseback.
They would soon make their
presence felt in Outremer.

The Ayubites were briefly united under al-Kamil, but chaos broke out after his death in 1238. The threats posed by Jelal ad-Din were removed by a greater one, as the unknown terror-to-come, the Mongols, further penetrated his eastern borders. The peace between Frederick and al-Kamil came to an end and a small crusading force, led by Tibald of Champagne and the duke of Burgundy, prompted by the pope, arrived in Acre in 1239. Apart from their involvement in the recovery of Ascalon on the coast, and some banditry, little was achieved. Tibald returned to Europe the following year with most of his men. The Templars and Hospitalers fell out once again; this time to the extent that physical violence occurred between the members of the two orders when they met in public. Both were resented by

▲ The al-Aqsa mosque in Jerusalem, the third holiest site in Islam.

the commoners as each operated without control, pursuing schemes that often ended with as many Christian deaths as Muslim. The continued absence of Conrad pushed the barons finally to appoint Alice and her husband, Ralph, as regents, until the day should come when Conrad would sail out to claim his kingdom. It was hoped that this would bring some degree of stability. The reality was that the regents had no control over the barons who had selected them. The military orders continued to scheme, the Templars replacing their previous policy with a new one of intervention in Muslim politics. At first their efforts were handsomely rewarded when they won back the Temple from the Muslims through cunning negotiation. Made overconfident by their success, they then tried to intercede in a war between two Muslim princes.

Ayub, the leader out of Egypt against whom the Templars had schemed, had his own plan to repay the interference. Since Jelal ad-Din's death his Khwarismian Turks had meandered throughout the region, indulging in sporadic pillaging. Ayub wrote to them, offering them Jerusalem and the surrounding areas. Ten thousand armed horsemen responded to his invitation. Thus was Jerusalem finally lost, in 1244. The refugees poured out and tried to make their way westward. Few escaped the depredations of the bandits who roamed the paths to the Frankish coast.

Meanwhile the cream of the Frankish forces sallied out to meet their Muslim allies. Together they met Ayub's army, strengthened by the Khwarismian Turks, outside the village of La Forbie. The Franks had backed the wrong side and were devastated in the ensuing battle. In a later incident the Khwarismian Turks turned against Ayub and were similarly destroyed. It was cold comfort for the Franks. Ayub's position was unchallenged in the Islamic world and he could turn his attention to the Franks who had dared to scheme against him. For now, he was content to level Ascalon after a siege.

In 1248, under the command of King Louis IX of France, a man revered for his piety, the forces of the Seventh Crusade arrived at Cyprus. This Crusade was very much a one-man affair. While the papacy was supportive of the endeavor, its main concern at that time was keeping Frederick in check. After much deliberation, the decision was made to strike at the heart of Ayub's kingdom: Egypt. The Crusaders arrived there in 1249 and, with admirable speed, captured Damietta. The rising floodwaters of the Nile delayed them for a few months and, when the Crusaders tried to push

▼ St. Louis, King Louis IX of France, depicted here with the symbols of the Crucifixion.

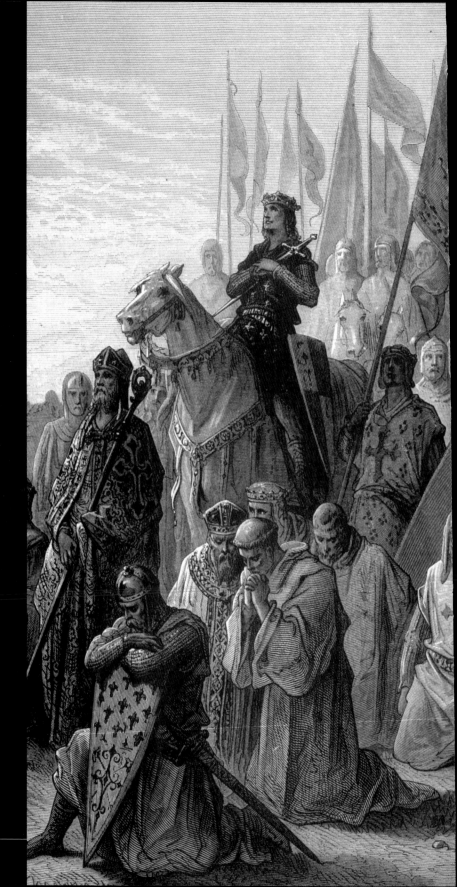

▷ Led by Louis, a Crusader army advances on Damietta, not for the first time.

south, they found a Muslim army ready to oppose them. The two armies hesitated for some time. When they finally clashed, outside the town of al-Mansura, the Crusader victory was bought with the lives of many of their men. The Muslims had punished them with their elite mercenary force, the Mameluks, who drove the Christians back when they tried to break into the town itself. By then Ayub had died of natural causes, after an offer of Jerusalem in exchange for Damietta—an offer that Louis rejected, much as Pelagius had before him.

Ayub's son, Turanshah, had not yet arrived to take command when the Muslims struck at the Crusaders once again. Louis' forces held out. It was clear, however, that the losses sustained in both battles would prevent them pressing further with the Crusade.

▲ Louis goes into battle against the Saracens on the Nile.

An attempt to retreat went badly wrong. The Muslims struck once more, this time capturing more prisoners than they knew what to do with, including the saintly but hapless Louis. When the huge ransom for the king had been paid, Louis departed for Outremer, awaiting the release of the rest of his companions, while many of those freed with him went back to France. Turanshah was dead, having been killed in a coup carried out by his Mameluk officers.

Louis stayed in Outremer until 1254, doing what he could before departing for France. Afterward, there was an internal struggle that outdid the brawling between the military orders. In 1256, competition between Genoa and Venice erupted into armed confrontation. This carried on for years, dragging in most of the barons of the region. Beyond Outremer, in Constantinople, the Venetians controlled trade. As a consequence, the Genoese supplied aid to the Nicaean Byzantine emperor, Michael Paleologus, in his attempts to recapture the city and the old empire. He succeeded in 1261 and the Genoese reaped the commercial rewards of a trading monopoly.

Outremer struggled on in increasing disarray. No more Crusades would be sent out from Europe. The Mongols were beginning to make their presence felt. They had already wiped out the Assassins in their Persian headquarters in 1257. In 1258, they sacked Baghdad, with a loss of eighty thousand lives. Christians rejoiced at the news yet they were uncertain about would happen when the Mongols finally reached the Levantine coast. The devastation that they had caused in Europe some 20 years earlier—getting as far as the Adriatic—was at the back of Frankish minds. The Mongols pushed on westward. Many Muslim lords were disposed to pay them homage once it became known what happened to those who

▲ Louis, represented as a saint with a halo, is captured by the Muslims while retreating.

▶ Baghdad is conquered by the Mongols, with the aid of a pontoon bridge and a siege engine.

refused. The prince of Mayyafaraqin was one of those who failed to pay. When the Mongols captured his city they killed him by forcing him to eat his own flesh. When they reached Antioch, the Christians paid the Mongol leader, Hulagu, due deference and were repaid by the restoration of territories previously won from the Franks by the Muslims. The Christians were jubilant. In 1260, Damascus had no alternative but to go over to the Mongols. News that Christians had accompanied the Mongol army from Antioch and Armenia when it rode into the city percolated through the Arab world. It was one more thing to hold against the Christians.

▶ Baibars sells captive Frankish women and children at a slave market after the fall of Antioch.

The final confrontation came that year, at Ain Jalud. Word that the Mongol leadership and part of their army had been drawn back East to resolve a question of succession gave the Muslims one last chance. A Mameluk army came out of Egypt to confront the Mongols. Everything was at stake. If they lost, then the Mongols could have ridden all the way to Morocco before encountering opposition. The whole future of Islam lay in the balance.

The Battle of Ain Jalud was hard fought but, at the end, the Muslims, under Sultan Qutuz, prevailed. The tide had turned.

In what was becoming a tradition, Qutuz had little time to enjoy his role as savior of Islam. One of his lieutenants, Baibars, who had won respect at Ain Jalud, assassinated his master and assumed his role. The Franks would come to curse his name.

▲ The Mongol ruler Hulagu interns the caliph of Baghdad among his treasures, with the intention of starving him to death.

9 The Fall of Acre and Afterward

IN THE AFTERMATH OF THE DEFEAT OF THE SEVENTH CRUSADE, WHAT REMAINED OF CHRISTENDOM IN THE EAST CAME UNDER REPEATED ASSAULT. THE TAKING OF THE CITY OF ACRE WAS A DEATH KNELL, SWIFTLY FOLLOWED BY THE FALL OF THE REMAINING CHRISTIAN STRONGHOLDS.

Introduction

Initially Baibars had to strengthen his own position in relation to the other Muslim leaders. Hulagu was still occupied in the East but it became clear that as many, if not more, Mongol leaders were converting to Islam as to Christianity. Factional squabbling among the Mongols strengthened Baibars' cause. He began to pick at Frankish territory. The town of Caesarea and the castle of Arsuf fell in 1265. The castle of Safed followed in 1266, the same year in which Baibars defeated the Armenians, paying them back for their support of the Mongols by destroying their capital and taking forty thousand prisoners. Baibars played a game of terror.

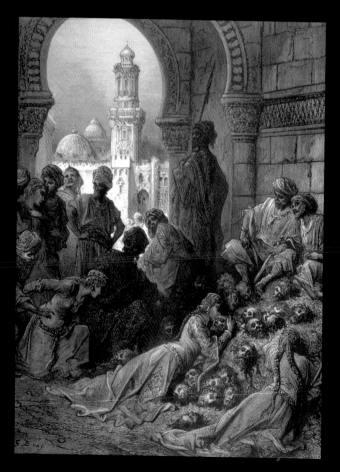

Truces were broken when he attacked those leaving a castle under the mistaken idea that they had been guaranteed safe passage. Captives were slaughtered, their skulls heaped in piles as proof of the fate awaiting those who displeased him. Throughout all this the coastal cities of Outremer still rang to the sound of Venetians setting on Genoese, and vice versa.

In 1268 Baibars finally had his revenge on those who had fought alongside the Armenians—the Christians of Antioch. The Mameluks killed or took as slaves all but the

◀ Crusader knights were ruthlessly butchered by Baibars in Antioch.

▲ The Crusader castle at Montfort, Israel, one of the finest examples of a fortified building in Outremer.

richest, whom they ransomed. The treasure taken was such that 'coins were so plentiful that they were handed out in bowlfuls."

Antioch was never the same again after this devastation. With its loss, the military orders surrendered the immediately surrounding castles and fortresses as they fled to safer ground. The remaining Assassins aligned themselves with Baibars' cause and he employed them with skill against the Christians. A small force arrived from Spain to help the Franks and then went back home again, having achieved nothing. Baibars continued to pick off Frankish and Templar and Hospitaler castles until Outremer was nothing more than a collection of scattered coastal fortresses. He now turned his attention back toward the Mongols. The Franks were a mere annoyance rather than a threat and, in 1271, his attention firmly on the East, Baibars agreed a ten-year truce with them.

The final retreat

Whether anything could have been made of this breathing space is purely speculative. In Europe the desperate situation in the East was noted and much commented upon yet no one would do anything practical about it. In Outremer the feuding continued between Venetians and Genoese and between Templars and Hospitalers. The reigning monarch, Hugh III, king of Jerusalem and Cyprus, became so tired of the infighting that he abandoned the mainland in 1276 and left for Cyprus. Initially he didn't even leave anyone else in charge in his absence.

The only good news for Europe was the death of Baibars in 1277. He was succeeded by Qalawun, who, by 1285, had started to carry on where Baibars had left off. He had negotiated a truce with part of Outremer in 1283 and, two years later, he was striking at the parts not covered by it. The Hospitaler castle at Marqab was taken first. Now the Pisans started on the Genoese. The prospects for Outremer

▼ The castle of the Knights Hospitaler at Marqab.

were so obviously bleak that even certain Mongols opposed to the Muslims sent an ambassador to Europe to plead for a new Crusade—with no success. Meanwhile, in 1287, Qalawun took Lattakieh. The Venetians and their allies went as far as to urge Qalawun to attack Tripoli so that they could take revenge on the Genoese there. In 1289 he readily complied and the destruction of Tripoli was complete. Qalawun killed all the men and enslaved the women and children. A few escaped to Cyprus, but others who tried to flee in small boats were slain in the surf where they were caught by the Mameluk horsemen. Qalawun leveled the city while the bodies rotted around it.

This dire news brought forth the faintest of responses from Europe. A rabble of drunks, peasants, and paupers was shipped from Italy by the Venetians. When they arrived at Acre they set upon the first Muslims they found, merchants and farmers identified as Muslim on the basis that they were the ones with beards. The thin truce that still held between Qalawun and Acre was torn up, such was Qalawun's anger. His death was the briefest of postponements. His dying words were commands to his son to carry on with his intention to take Acre.

Al-Ashraf kept the promise he made to his father. Over a hundred thousand men appeared outside Acre in 1291. Al-Ashraf brought with him a pair of huge catapults known as Victorious and Furious. Engineers worked to bring down the walls and a constant rain of arrows and crude bombs fell on the defenders within. Eventually, despite heroic resistance, the Mameluks broke through. The defenders, Templars, Hospitalers, and Franks, fought side by side as more and more of the enemy poured into the city. Though they were driven back toward the port their resistance provided others with sufficient time to take to the sea and flee.

By the time the Mameluks had finished, there were few live captives to send to the slave markets of the East. Again, as at Tripoli, al-Ashraf destroyed as much of the city as he could, determined that it could never be used again should the Christians ever attempt to return. This was in May and, by the middle of August, Tyre, Sidon, Beirut, and Haifa had all fallen. The last castles of the military orders had been evacuated. With the exception of the Templar castle on the tiny island of Ruad, just off the coast, the Franks had been wiped from the map of the East. Those few who escaped but were unable to find sanctuary in Europe, crowded into Cyprus as refugees.

None of them would ever return.

◀ William of Clermont's army fights to defend Acre against al-Ashraf's army in 1291.

Epilogue

ISLAM EVENTUALLY TRIUMPHED IN THE EAST IN 1453 WHEN CONSTANTINOPLE WAS CAPTURED AND THE BYZANTINE EMPIRE WAS FINALLY BROUGHT TO AN END. THE LONG ERA OF THE CRUSADES HAD ACHIEVED NOTHING OF VALUE, AND HAD SET THE SCENE FOR CENTURIES OF CONFRONTATION BETWEEN CHRISTIANITY AND ISLAM.

The end of the tale

All told, the Crusades had achieved very little. The financial cost and the loss of life on both sides were enormous. Only the Italian city-states benefited from the trading opportunities that were created. It may well be that this newfound wealth actually advanced the birth of the Renaissance in Italy.

The barbarities committed by the Franks inspired the same behavior from the Muslims, and the memory of the Frankish acts profoundly changed the relationship between Islam and Christianity, down to the present day. In the end the forces of Islam would triumph when Ottoman Turks emerged from a tiny area in Asia Minor. They rose to

▼ The leaders of the Order of Teutonic Knights, established In Acre by the Germans during the Third Crusade, using the Order of the Temple as a model.

◀ The interrogation of Jacques de Molay, Grand Master of the Knights Templar. He was burnt at the stake in 1314.

form an empire that eventually, in 1453, brought about the final end of the Byzantine Empire when they captured Constantinople. The empire they founded lasted until the early years of the twentieth century and they occupied the Balkans for centuries, in a reversal of the Christian occupation of the Holy Land. The Holy Land itself finally passed from the control of the Ottomans to the British in 1920 under the Treaty of Sèvres following the First World War. The state of Israel was created in 1948.

The Crusades continued in Europe, both in Livonia in the Baltic where the Teutonic Knights pursued the heathens for many years, and as a tool to strike against heretics within Europe. European struggles against the Turks in the succeeding centuries were still often seen and described as Crusades.

Not long after the fall of Acre the Templars were accused of blasphemy and their vast wealth was divided among the Hospitalers and the rulers who acquiesced in their prosecution. Their last Grand Master, Jacques de Molay, was burnt at the stake in 1314.

The Hospitalers preserved themselves by staying out of reach of avaricious kings, first in Rhodes, and then in Malta. Napoleon finally dislodged them from that island in 1798. Thereafter, they became a ceremonial order, still in existence today.

The Crusades became the stuff of legend in Europe. The exploits of the Crusader knights were celebrated in the Romantic period in painting and literature. The image persisted of the chivalrous knight, wearing a red cross, heroically doing battle with the Infidel.

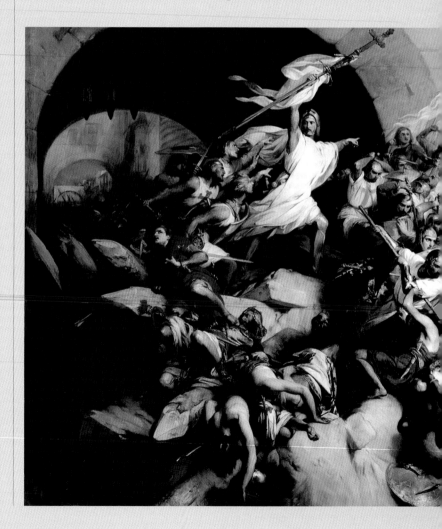

▶ A romanticized depiction of Rhodes being defended against Sultan Osman I by the Knights of St. John of Jerusalem.

Frederick II lost his struggle with the papacy; within 30 years of his death his heirs had lost the same battle. However, the German people never forgot him and he was revered for his exploits. Indeed, many believed that he was not dead but was merely asleep, and would awake to lead Germany again to glory, much as folk tales declared that the legendary King Arthur of Britain rested, waiting to come to the aid of his country in times of great trial.

▲ The romance of the Crusades caught the popular imagination for centuries, with works of art depicting brave knights setting out on their mission, encouraged by fair ladies.

Reference

Chronology

638	Capture of Jerusalem by Caliph Omar.
1095	Pope Urban II preaches the First Crusade at Clermont (November).
1096	Launch of the First Crusade. Two armies comprising the "People's Crusade," led by Peter the Hermit and Walter the Penniless, arrive in advance of the official armies led by a group of nobles, Raymond of Toulouse and Bohemond of Taranto senior among them.
1098	Edessa is captured (March).
	Antioch is captured (June).
1099	Jerusalem is captured (July).
1144	Fall of Edessa to Zangi (December). News in Europe of its fall provides the impetus for the Second Crusade.
1147	Launch of the Second Crusade by Pope Eugenius III, under the overall command of Louis VII of France and Conrad of Germany. Islamic forces are led by Zangi's son, Nur ed-Din.
1149	End of the Second Crusade.
1187	Battle of Hattin (July).
	Jerusalem falls to Saladin (October).
	Pope Gregory VIII calls for the Third Crusade in response. Three rulers—Richard I of England, Philip II of France, and Holy Roman Emperor Frederick I—take part, with their respective forces.
1190	Frederick I dies leading his army in Cilicia.
1191	Cyprus falls to Richard I.
	Acre falls to Richard I and Philip II.
1192	The Third Crusade ends with the Treaty of Jaffa.
1202	The Fourth Crusade finally gets under way, four years after its proclamation by Pope Innocent III.
	Zara is taken by the Crusaders from the Hungarians (November).

1204	Constantinople is sacked by Crusaders.
	End of the Fourth Crusade.
1212	The Children's Crusade.
1218	The Fifth Crusade. A motley army lands in Egypt under John of Brienne.
	Siege of Damietta.
1221	The Fifth Crusade ends, defeated by al-Kamil.
1228	The Sixth Crusade. Holy Roman Emperor Frederick II arrives in the Levant.
1229	Jerusalem is won back through Frederick II's diplomacy (February). The Crusade ends with his departure for Europe later that year.
1249	The Seventh Crusade, under Louis IX of France, lands in Egypt. Damietta is captured.
1250	The Seventh Crusade ends in defeat at al-Mansura. Louis stays on in Palestine for four years before returning home.
1258	Mongols sack Baghdad.
1260	Battle of Ain Jalud—the Mongols are defeated by the Mameluks.
1268	Antioch is captured by the Mameluks.
	The last remaining Frankish territory (including Acre and Beirut) in the East falls to the Islamic forces under Qalawun.

Bibliography

Ambrosini, M. L., *The Secret Archives of the Vatican,* London: Little Brown & Co., 1970

Barber, Malcolm, *Crusaders and Heretics 12th–14th Centuries,* Aldershot: Ashgate, 1995

Christiansen, Eric, *The Northern Crusades,* 2nd ed., London: Penguin Books 1998

Ehrenkreuz, Andrew S., *Saladin,* Albany: State University of New York, 1972

Gibbon, Edward, *The History of the Decline and Fall of the Roman Empire,* London: Penguin Books, 2003

Harris, Jonathan, *Byzantium and the Crusades,* London: Hambledon & London, 2003

Hillenbrand, C., *The Crusades: Islamic Perspectives,* Edinburgh: Edinburgh University Press, 1999

Housley, Norman, *The Later Crusades, 1274–1580,* Oxford: Oxford University Press, 1992

Joinville and Villehardouin, *Chronicles of the Crusades,* London: Penguin Books, 1970

Maalouf, Amin, ed., *The Crusades through Arab Eyes,* London & New York: Schocken, 1984

Newby, P.H., *Saladin in His Time,* London: Faber & Faber, 1983; New York: Dorset Press, 1992

Nicholson, Helen, *Templars, Hospitallers, and Teutonic Knights: Images of the Military Orders, 1128–1291,* Leicester: Leicester University Press, 1993

Oldenbourg, Zoë, *The Crusades,* London: Phoenix, 2001

Partner, P., *The Knights Templar and Their Myth,* Rochester VT: Destiny Books, 1990

Phillips, Jonathan, *The Fourth Crusade and the Sack of Constantinople,* London: Pimlico, 2005

Ralls, K., *The Knights Templar Encyclopaedia,* Franklin Lakes NJ: Career Press 2007

Richard, Jean, *The Crusades,* Cambridge: Cambridge University Press, 1999

Riley-Smith, Jonathan, ed., *The Oxford History of the Crusades,* Oxford: Oxford University Press, 1995

Runciman, S., *A History of the Crusades,* 3 vols., London: Penguin Books, 1978

Setton, K.M., ed., *A History of the Crusades*, 2nd ed., 6 vols., Madison, Wis.: 1969–89

Sumption, Jonathan, *The Albigensian Crusade,* London: Faber & Faber, 1999

Tyerman, Christopher, *God's War,* London: Penguin Books, 2006

Wasserman, James, *The Templars and the Assassins: The Militia of Heaven,* Rochester: Inner Traditions, 2001

Watson, William, *The Last of the Templars,* London: The Harvill Press, 1992

Index